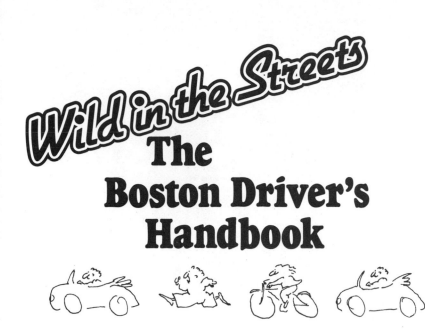

Wild in the Streets
The Boston Driver's Handbook

Ira Gershkoff
and
Richard Trachtma

Addison-Wesley Publishing Company, Inc.

Reading, Massachusetts • Menlo Park, California • New York
Don Mills, Ontario • Wokingham, England • Amsterdam
Sydney • Singapore • Tokyo • Madrid • Bogotá
Santiago • San Juan

Library of Congress Cataloging in Publication Data

Gershkoff, Ira.
　The Boston driver's handbook.

　　1. Automobile driving—Massachusetts—Boston.
I. Trachtman, Richard.　II. Title.
TL152.52.G47　1982　　629.28'32'0974461　　82-8692
ISBN 0-201-11000-8 (pbk.)　　　　　　　　　　　AACR2

Copyright © 1982 by Ira Gershkoff and Richard Trachtman.

Library of Congress Catalog Card No. 82-8692.

ISBN 0-201-11000-8

IJKLMNOPQR-DO-8987

Cover illustration by Chris Demarest.

Maneuver illustrations by Pamela Cass Gershkoff.
Other illustrations by Chris Demarest.

Ninth Printing, July 1987

CONTENTS

CHAPTER ONE

Getting started

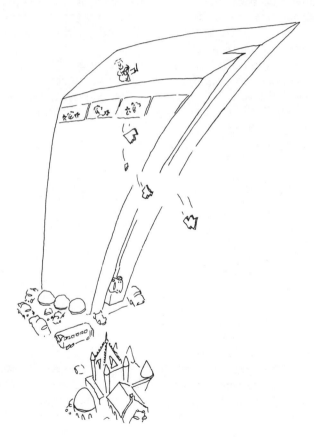

The Philosophy of Boston Driving

There is perhaps only one place where it is socially acceptable for a human being to give in to all of his primal urges while driving an automobile: Boston, Massachusetts. Whether it be a cleverly executed U-turn into a lonely parking space or just a routine left turn from the right lane of a busy street, the craft and artistry of a Boston Driver is a sight to behold, preferably at a safe distance. In Boston itself, one need only look to the nearest street corner to witness the crumbling of the stop sign barrier or perhaps hear the delicate crunch of a fenderbender. No one really seems to mind, least of all the Boston Police. In New England's largest city, Boston Drivers, and their antics, are inescapable.

This book is about the world of Boston Driving, a fascinating sport currently practiced by nearly two million licensed drivers in one of America's largest cities. You will find Boston Driving to be full of challenge and highly competitive. It's a dog-eat-dog situation: if you don't look out for Number One, at best you'll be left far, far behind.

At worst, you may be tempted to bury your car in a pothole and turn in your license. The sport has spread to other cities, but at this time no other city can come close to matching the caliber of Boston's own Boston Drivers.

In this book we will discuss the offensive driving skills you will need to know to ensure your survival as a motorist here. We will lead you step-by-step from basic

techniques such as the Cutoff and Sidesqueeze through the more advanced maneuvers involving turns through gas stations or sidewalk driving. We will also cover the proper Boston handling of common hazards such as pedestrians, potholes, and cab drivers. For those who are not intimately familiar with the Boston area, we will cover the city's street design, focusing on the particular problems of getting around and parking in specific neighborhoods.

However, before we can go any further, we must set forth the First Commandment of Boston Driving:

Thou shalt reach thy destination as quickly as possible. Everyone and everything else be damned.

Every lane change, maneuver, turn, acceleration, or deceleration is made with this ultimate goal in mind. Trivial socioeconomic considerations such as gas mileage, wear and tear on the car, and especially safety are to be ignored. Let's face it: "defensive driving" is an auto insurance company conspiracy and has no place in Boston Driving. The only things that count are arrival and survival.

Keep this goal in mind as you read this book. And remember, every driving maneuver is just a logical extension of the Boston Driving philosophy. The most important car on the road is *your* car. *You* come first, *always.* No special skills are required to become a first-rate Boston Driver; it is only necessary to have the proper attitude. If nothing else, keep that in mind, and you'll never go too far wrong.

Good luck!

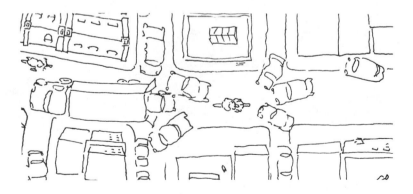

The WRONG kind of car for Boston Driving.
1978 Chevrolet Corvette

The RIGHT kind of car for Boston Driving.
1965 Ford Falcon

A. Semi-bald snow tires; B. Wire holding door closed; C. Coat hangar radio antenna; D. Liberal rust; E. Fender-bender dents; and F. Deluxe wheel covers.

About Your Car

A car is the most important piece of equipment you will need for Boston Driving. You should choose one carefully since your car will determine to some extent which maneuvers you can or cannot perform.

Small cars are preferable to large because they handle better and are more maneuverable. They are also much easier to park. On the other hand, larger cars are better for hogging the road, if you are so inclined. Good acceleration and braking capabilities are assets for any car, small or large. You will often need them for cutting off other cars in heavy traffic.

It is always a good idea to have a few dents strategically placed around the car's body. The advantages are many. First, if you already have some dents, you won't worry about getting a few more. There is no surer way of getting involved in a fender-bender than worrying about getting involved in a fender-bender. Second, dents make your car a less attractive target for Boston's prolific car thieves. If they have a choice between your '71 Pinto and the brand new Porsche parked next to you, guess who's going to get hit. Finally, when other drivers see your dents, they assume you have been in a number of accidents. They figure you are a lousy driver, probably a little bit drunk and crazy as well. Your insurance was probably canceled long ago, they figure, so why should they risk life, limb, and property messing with you? Dents do wonders to clear the roadway around you.

It follows that a new car is the *worst* kind of car for Boston Driving. You will naturally worry about cracking it up, so you will. Other drivers will take advantage of you unmercifully. Your car will be a prime target for theft. The new car condition is self-curing, however. Sooner or later your new car will receive its proper Boston baptism. After it has been stolen a few times and has caught a few nicks and scrapes banging up cars and pedestrians, it will no longer be new, and you won't have to worry about it anymore.

One other point on theft is worth mentioning. Boston is the car theft capital of the world, but the average thief is fourteen years old and needs a car only to take him to the next car that he will steal. Life being this way, you should make your car as unattractive as possible to the average fourteen-year-old boy. This means no mag wheels, CB radios, racing stripes, or tape decks, and absolutely nothing bigger than a nickel in plain slight.

If you were a fourteen-year-old car thief, you wouldn't steal just any car; you'd want to exhibit a certain amount of taste. So you'd look for a car with lots of chrome and glitter and enough power to chase a 747, like a high-powered late model American sports car. You'd also want to sit in air-conditioned comfort (even in the winter) listening to your favorite top-40 station on your victim's (hopefully) expensive stereo system. From a theft standpoint, therefore, the ideal car to own is a beat-up American subcompact with at least 50,000 miles on it, semi-bald tires, and liberal rust on its body.

Honor thy vehicle—and keep it "holey."

License and Registration

A necessary step for becoming a card-carrying Boston Driver is to make a trip down to the Registry of Motor Vehicles at 100 Nashua Street, just a few blocks from North Station. Grab a parking space anywhere in the vicinity; if you're lucky, you might avoid having to park in the filth underneath the elevated subway tracks. Then go inside, get in line, and wait. And wait. And wait some more. It is advisable to bring along extra food and water for this long siege. (You might also bring along this book so you can read up on what to do when you finally do get out, to make up for lost time.) Though the wait seems endless, sooner or later (most likely later) you will get to the front of the line and get what you came for.

Inspection

Before you can legally launch your heap into the cold cruel world of the streets of Boston, you are supposed to have it inspected. If you don't have a valid inspection sticker, the chances are that you will get a ticket for it sooner or later. And after several tickets your pride and joy will be unceremoniously towed away. So unless you are in a belligerent mood, you will have to have an inspection sticker.

To get your sticker you will have to go to one of the Authorized Inspection Stations in the metropolitan area. Generally, the attendant will eyeball your car, kick the tires, and give you your sticker. If he starts getting serious by approaching the hood, this is the time to become very friendly and start making conversation. If it's spring inspection, ask him if he thinks Jim Rice will hit forty home runs this year. If it's autumn, ask him if he thinks the Bruins can catch Montreal. This should soften him up. If all else fails, greasing his palm with an extra couple of bucks should bring his attitude around to your way of thinking.

Insurance

Massachusetts has been long famous for having one of the highest auto insurance rates in the nation. There is good reason for this. Massachusetts has the worst kept roads (see Chapter IV, "Potholes"), the loosest traffic law enforcement, the most skillful car thieves, and the highest number of accidents per capita of any state (i.e., the worst drivers). If these conditions continue to hold—and there is every reason to expect them to do so—there will be no relief in sight. Let's face it: driving in Massachusetts, especially Boston, is like driving the bumper cars at an amusement park (also known as "dodgems"). You don't have to pay attention to the condition of your already beat-up car; try not to get hit, but don't worry if you are.

Auto insurance is supposed to spread the cost of accidents over all motorists, but it frequently doesn't quite work out that way. Massachusetts requires a minimum of $5,000 insurance for injury to one person and $10,000 insurance for total damages resulting from an accident. But everyone knows that at current levels of auto repair costs, lawyers' fees, and especially medical expenses, $5,000/$10,000 won't buy a band-aid.

It is the same story with collision insurance, although collision is not legally required. Collision insurance is designed to protect against loss in the value of your car due to an accident, but most cars still alive after three years on the streets of Boston have nothing left worth insuring for collision anyway. In many cases, collision insurance will cost more than 100 percent of the book value of the car, a guaranteed losing proposition.

Over the years, the Massachusetts state legislature has originated many innovative approaches to the auto insurance problem, some of which have been adopted by other states. In 1973 Massachusetts became the first state to enact a "no-fault" law. All auto accidents with less than $2,000 in property damage and no bodily injury claims were to be settled for each involved driver by his or her own insurance company. For a year or two, the system worked beautifully. But Massachusetts drivers eventually turned out to be much more innovative than the laws which regulate them. Thirty dollars' worth of bent fender tended to show up as $600 worth of body work on the estimate, and the motorist would pocket the difference, possibly including a gratuity to the body shop owner. (In recent years, some insurance companies have responded to this ploy by hiring their own appraisers and negotiating directly with the body shop.) The state has now instituted a merit rating system, which is designed to impose a surcharge on insurance for those drivers involved in accidents or traffic violations and distribute the funds to the "good" drivers. Rest assured that it is only a matter of time before Massachusetts drivers find a way to beat this one, too.

[12]

The Law—and How Little It Means to You

A real collector's item among Boston Drivers is an authentic, bonafide moving violation. An acquaintance of ours drove the wrong way down Boylston Street from the Public Garden all the way to the Prudential Center before being stopped by the police. They informed him that the "preferred direction" was the other way and sent him along. On another occasion, while drunk on a snowy winter's night, our friend sideswiped three parked cars on Beacon Street. The police gave him a *warning* for not having snow tires, as is required by law during snow emergencies.

The only way you really have a good chance for a moving violation is to hit something that can vote. Then you'll probably get several moving violations, and your friends will be eternally jeal-ous. Any other maneuver, no matter how blatantly illegal, hasn't got a prayer. Speeding, going the wrong way down a one way street, illegal turns, obstructing traffic, and all those other violations that fill the law books are a waste of time because you just won't stand out from the crowd of your fellow lawbreaking Boston Drivers.

The only exception that we know of is that the state troopers occasionally become rather sensitive about enforcing the 55 m.p.h. speed limit on the Mass. Pike. This usually comes about as a result of periodic pressure from Washington for Massachusetts to show that it is really doing what it can to conserve energy. One way to "prove" this is to enforce the 55 m.p.h. speed limit. After a couple of weeks things usually return to normal.

Safety Considerations in Boston Driving

None.

Speaking the Language

The newcomer to Boston is always impressed by the dialect spoken here. Westerners think they are in a foreign country; Midwesterners are tolerant; Southerners fall in love with it; Washingtonians turn up their noses; and New Yorkers and Philadelphians laugh out loud when they hear it. Yes indeed, it really is English they're speaking, but you have to keep your ears wide open and remember a few translation rules.

Pronunciation may best be characterized as lazy. Bostonians don't like to finish off their words; speech is somewhat slurred as one word rolls awkwardly into the next. Properly done, Bostonese is louder and

coarser than normal English. The biggest problem for the novice is the pathetic pronunciation of the letter R, especially at the end of a word or syllable. For example:

AR is pronounced "ah"
(pahk the cah)

ER is pronounced "uh"
(what a muhthuh)

OR is pronounced "aw"
(give it maw gas)

ERS is pronounced "iz"
(watch those Boston driviz)

To give you an idea of what to expect, we turn to noted citizen and part-time MBTA bus driver Harry ("High-Gear") Harrison,

for a testimonial on the relative advantages of the Massachusetts turnpike over alternate roads:

The pike shuah is fast, but geez, it is expensive. You get on by the rivvuh theyuh, ya know, neah Cambridge, and take it out to route one-twenny-eight, and it'll costya the bettuh paht of a dollah. And at rush houah, especially on Frideez, the cahs sometimes back up cleah to Hahvuhd Squeyuh. I guess ya haffta take it if yaw headed faw New Yawk uh Hahtfuhd aw sump'm, but if yaw goin to Concuhd aw nawth to New Hampshuh aw some place like that, I'm shuah you could find a bettuh way.

And Finally. . .

You now should have all the necessary hardware to learn how to become a full-fledged Boston Driver. You have a car, license, registration, inspection, and insurance. You also know how to communicate with the natives. Add a little common sense, and you would have enough to drive anywhere—anywhere except

Boston, that is. Only after you read the rest of this book can you claim to have the proper qualifications to reach your destination in minimum time and truly enjoy the sport of Boston Driving.

CHAPTER TWO

Street layout

With its deep water harbor and access to two navigable rivers (Charles and Mystic), Boston was a natural spot to build a city back in the seventeenth century, when those things mattered. Surrounded on three sides by water, the city's limited access to the mainland made it relatively easy to defend against Indians, French, or other hostile forces. One is not likely to find the layout of the streets of greater Boston quite so natural. The hodgepodge of one and two way streets pointing in different directions, curving wildly, merging from three lanes to one and back again, and sprinkled with "No Left Turn" signs, is enough to unsettle any anarchist. In this chapter we will attempt to unravel the mystery somewhat by presenting a few useful pointers in getting around the city.

Boston's City "Plan"

The most widely accepted theory on the nonsense of Boston street layout is known as the Cow Pasture Theory. To understand it, one must again return to seventeenth-century Boston. In those days, residents liked to graze their cows on the Common and do a little socializing at the same time. On the often roundabout way to and from their barns, the cows would make paths. The biggest of these became Beacon Street; Tremont, Washington, and all the rest followed. The reason Boston's streets are what they are today, so the theory goes, is that they were designed by cows, and the cows were simply not clever enough to envision the coming of the automobile 250 years later when deciding where to make their tracks.

This theory also explains the development of all the squares and circles in the city. With so many cowpaths intersecting at a variety of angles, squares and circles naturally developed. Many were used as meeting places for the Pilgrims long before the days of Paul Revere, New England clam chowder, and the Boston Red Sox. However they came about, there is no rhyme or reason to the location, frequency, or density of squares. To this day, Boston remains a place where the unsuspecting motorist can drive in circles for hours while trying to go between squares.

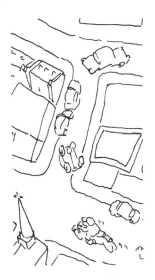

Another, less popular rumor has it that the city planner back in those days had a soft spot for Italian food, and he saw the street plan one day in his bowl of spaghetti. While this theory does not have the following of the Cow Pasture Theory, it nevertheless could well explain the random development of the street layout. Looking at a map of Boston, one can see the great appeal in this explanation.

The point of this discussion is that there is no substitute in Boston Driving for a thorough knowledge of the roads. Knowing which lane to ride in or where to turn in certain situations is a key factor in executing many maneuvers. Also good to know are shortcuts through residential areas, pothole locations, and traffic light cycles.

If you are in an unfamiliar part of town, don't even try to navigate by street signs. Most intersections don't have them; those that do are likely to be turned. Major streets are almost never marked; cross streets might be, but the information seldom will do you any good. It is assumed that the motorist always knows which street he is driving on. Since even experienced Boston Drivers do not always know this, and since there is no logic to the layout of the streets, getting lost is a common occurrence.

Thou shalt ever resist the temptation to put thy trust in street signs.

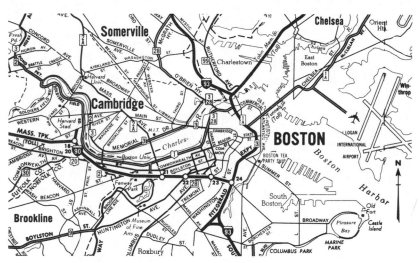

Boston Street Layout.

Major Neighborhoods

Downtown

The downtown area consists of most of the land between the Boston Common and the Central Artery. It includes Government Center, the financial district, the Downtown Crossing and other shopping areas, the Combat Zone, and Chinatown. It is one of the oldest sections of the city. Streets are usually narrow and almost always one way, and pedestrians outnumber cars at least twenty to one. Don't worry if you get lost: because of the cow pasture layout, you'll end up back where you started before you know it. It is the most congested part of the city, and there just isn't much room for cars. Traffic is terrible all the time, and the pedestrians will harass you to boot. We do not recommend motoring in this part of town unless absolutely necessary.

Back Bay

About a hundred years ago, Boston embarked on a number of land reclamation projects. The largest of these is now known as Back Bay, so called because it was originally a shallow marsh that would flood at high tide. The mouth of the Charles River was then in the vicinity of the current B.U. Bridge. Because of its relative youth, most of the original townhouses built on the reclaimed land are still standing and in use.

Furthermore, Back Bay shocks us with its parallel streets intersecting at right angles. To add still more sanity, the streets are in alphabetical order. Any seasoned Boston Driver can rattle them off for you: Arlington, Berekely, Clarendon, Dartmouth, Exeter, Fairfield, Gloucester, and Hereford. Most people don't know that the streets continue after Massachusetts Avenue: Ipswich, Jersey, and Kilmarnock.

The street closest to the Charles River is called Back Street, aptly named because it faces the rear of the even-numbered houses on Beacon Street. Drivers sometimes take Back Street to avoid the traffic on Beacon or Marlborough Streets. However, it is used

Back Street.

mainly for parking, garbage pickup (and occasionally dumping), and committing violent crimes. Garbage scavengers, car thieves, muggers, and murderers flourish in this isolated environment. Incredibly, Back Street is two-way, and it is often difficult for two cars to get by each other. Somehow this has had little effect on the tow trucks which are the mainstay of Back Street's economy. They always have plenty to do, for there is no public parking permitted on Back Street.

Beacon Hill

Another part of Boston that dates to colonial times is the Beacon Hill section. It is roughly the area enclosed by Charles, Beacon, and Cambridge Streets. This neighborhood is characterized by small, expensive townhomes and narrow, hilly streets. Because of the nostalgic atmosphere and the proximity to downtown Boston, Beacon Hill is an "in" place to live.

Driving through Beacon Hill is another matter, however. It can be difficult to maneuver through this area because of the narrow, one-way streets, many of which are on especially steep inclines as well. Because Charles Street is one way toward the Longfellow Bridge, traveling from the Bridge to the downtown area through Beacon Hill is quite a challenge. It can be done, but it takes a lot of trial and error to learn the route through the labyrinth of crisscrossing one-way streets. To make things even worse, the "preferred" direction of certain streets has been known to have been suddenly reversed on occasion.

Gas lamps still function on some streets on Beacon Hill, and many streets are cobblestoned to this day. On some street corners, lit red globes indicate the presence of a fire alarm. We know of one poor soul who encountered one of these red globes one night when he had had a few too many. Thinking he was in the presence of a red traffic light, our hero patiently waited for it to turn green. For all we know, he is still waiting.

North End

The North End is an old, predominately Italian part of town. (This is where "Wednesday is Prince Spaghetti Day" came from.) Like Beacon Hill, streets are narrow and occasionally cobblestoned. In addition, the many fine restaurants of the area bring on a high incidence of double parking. Because of the combination of double parking and narrow streets, don't be surprised to find that the street you are on is unnavigable.

Residents of the North End are fiercely loyal, pro-union Americans, and foreign cars are treated accordingly. Tire-slashing and window-breaking on imported cars are popular pastimes here. Cars with out-of-state plates have been known to be given the same type of North End "visitor's welcome". Conversely, shiny black Cadillacs with Massachusetts tags are treated with the utmost respect.

Standard procedure for the North End "enforcers" is to break into a car, swipe whatever personal property is found, sort through it, and discard any unwanted merchandise at the end of Stillman Street, underneath the Central Artery. Other, less popular dumping grounds can be found at the alley on Endicott Street and the junction of Salem and Prince Streets. If you have to bring a high-risk car into the North End, make sure you have kept up on your protection payments.

Waterfront

The waterfront area runs along Atlantic Avenue between the North End and South Station. For the last several years it has been the most rapidly developing area of Boston; luxury high-rise apartments now stand where dilapidated warehouses used to be. The revitalized Faneuil Hall, which borders the waterfront area, has been immensely popular among residents and tourists alike.

These tourists (and their cars) are the primary source of trouble for the Waterfront Boston Drivers. You can spot them easily by their out-of-state plates, their unusually fresh-looking cars (provided this is their first day in town), and the bewildered look on their faces as they struggle to make sense of the street layout of Boston. Because of their lack of knowledge on the rules of the road for Boston Drivers, they can be very erratic and unpredictable.

For the same reason, however, you will find tourists easy to take advantage of. For some reason they have a lot of trouble navigating along the frequent curves on Atlantic Avenue. Apparently they are worried that one false move will send them over the edge of the nearest wharf into the murky waters of Boston Harbor. They also seem to be intimidated by the presence of the elevated Central Artery passing through the waterfront area. When crossing underneath it, they drive as though they are worried about being hit topside by an airborne car which had attempted unsuccessfully to pass a truck on the expressway above.

Allston/Brighton

Although the physical layout of the streets of Allston/Brighton is not particularly threatening, this area boasts the most aggressive, arrogant, and selfish drivers in the Boston area. Here are the cream of the crop: the most Boston of Boston Drivers.

Out-of-state plates are common in Allston/Brighton, as the area has a predominantly student population. Many residents are young and transient; most of their cars are old and veterans of many a fenderbender. New cars are seldom seen since few residents are rich enough to afford a full-time bodyguard for their car, and without one, a new car becomes indistinguishable from the masses within a week.

Commonwealth Avenue in Allston/Brighton is unique among the streets of Boston in that it has six lanes of traffic, two lanes of trolley tracks, and three medians. Two of the lanes are given to a service road otherwise known as "Parking Lot Row." It is unclear for what use these lanes were intended, but they do provide the only on-street parking for Commonwealth Avenue. They extend about three miles from Brighton Avenue all the way to Chestnut Hill Avenue. The only reason to travel in these roads is if you want to park. If you try to travel in these lanes, you will be hung up by drivers pulling in and out of spaces, looking for spaces, double-parking, or talking to their friends. In the winter these roads are never plowed, so you might end up getting stuck or at least have to help push someone out of a drift. At cross streets it is often difficult to turn from Parking Lot Row to the main part of Commonwealth Avenue, and a left turn is a real challenge.

A former new car from Allston/Brighton.

Brighton Intersection Dynamics

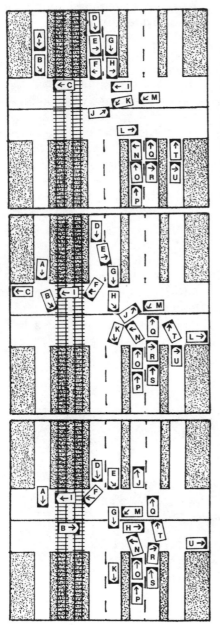

The light has just turned yellow on Harvard Street (left to right). C and I are proceeding through the intersection on Harvard St. toward Allston. L is going the opposite way, toward Brookline. M and K are trying to turn left onto Commonwealth Avenue outbound; J is trying to turn inbound. All other drivers are waiting for the Comm. Ave. light to turn green. E is trying his left turn from the right lane: difficult, but by no means unusual. Relatively speaking, the situation is quite calm.

Things begin to pick up, as B enters the intersection for a left turn. C escapes to Allston. D waits as E changes lanes for left turn. F begins right turn but must stop, as I is cut off by B. G follows H, which must go around J, who is waiting to take a left. K takes her left and is on her way toward Brighton; L proceeds to Brookline. M must wait for J; N for K; O and P must wait for N; and R and S must wait for T, who is trying to get on the main part of Comm. Ave. from Parking Lot Row. T yields to Q, who is waiting for M to take his left, and U will wait for T, then follow L.

Congestion reaches a peak, as B sees enough daylight to take his left, allowing A into the intersection just in time to cut off I. F begins his right turn behind I, but does not get far enough for D to proceed. E and M are blocked by G, who in turn is cut off by N continuing her left turn in the wrong lane. H must wait for T, who is following Q. O and P are still waiting for N to get out of the way, and R and S are waiting for T. J, K, Q, and U have clear sailing.

Brighton Intersection Dynamics (continued)

Action finally begins to subside. A crosses intersection, allowing I and F a clear road to Allston. B continues toward Brookline, but is cut off by G, who is still waiting for N. N must continue in the wrong lane around B. D is stymied when he reaches B. E, frustrated by now, begins his turn by going in the wrong lane around M the way N is going around B. M is still waiting for G. H could go, but R took his turn wide and cut him off. O, P, and S are still waiting for the intersection to clear. J, Q, and T travel on unimpeded.

N continues in the wrong lane, allowing G to break into the clear. This allows B to move forward a few feet and lets D move on. E continues in the wrong lane, planning to move in behind H and R. Poor M continues to wait for his break, and holds up O, P, and S. A, F, and T leave the scene.

The intersection is nearly clear when the Commonwealth Avenue light turns yellow. B must wait for O and P to cross the intersection. When B goes by, M can take his left. (Note that M sat in the intersection for the entire light cycle. Had M been as good a Boston Driver as N, this never would have happened.) N and E are making their way back to the right side of the street. Everyone else has an unobstructed path.

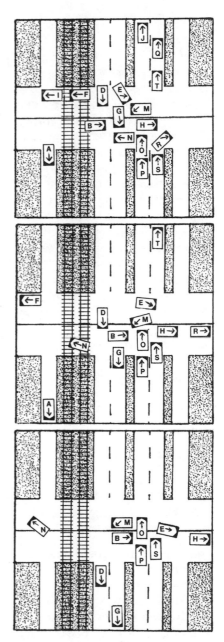

Cambridge

Seat of two of the world's foremost universities, Cambridge is not very enlightened on the subject of street layout. The Cow Pasture Theory holds up very well here, as Harvard, Central, Tech, Kendall, Porter, Inman, and Lechmere Squares testify. All these squares have numerous streets coming together at the intersection, resulting in frequent traffic bottlenecks. Cambridge was the originator of the "one way the wrong way" maneuver (see Chapter III, "One-way Streets"). This was born out of necessity; with the long, narrow one-way streets, it would be too much to expect anyone to take the trouble to go around.

A discussion of street layout in Cambridge must center around Massachusetts Avenue, the principal thoroughfare and lifeblood of this city. Seldom less than four lanes wide, it passes through nearly all of the commercial areas of the city and is within walking distance of almost every resident.

Traffic along Mass. Ave. can be incredibly dense and move unbearably slowly. A relentless string of traffic lights will dot your path, and pedestrians can usually move faster than cars. Whenever possible, keep to the middle of Mass. Ave. Too far right will find you waiting for buses, double-parked cars, and people looking for parking. Too far left, and you will be behind cars attempting left turns. If there are only two lanes, stay alert and play it by ear.

Major Roads

Central Artery/Southeast Expressway

This road is the granddaddy of Boston expressways, and it looks it. The expressway extends from the North Station area all the way to Route 128 in Braintree (the Central Artery officially merges with the Southeast Expressway near the South Station area in Boston). Originally designed for 75,000 cars per day, it is ill-equipped to handle the daily burden of about twice that figure. More people come in and out of Boston on the Southeast Expressway than on any other road. Numerous large, slow-moving trucks contribute their foul exhaust to this already over-crowded and overpolluted high-

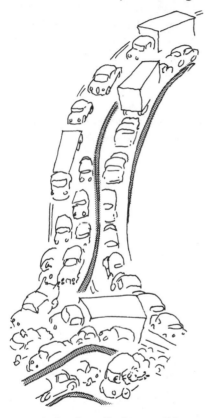

way. It is virtually impossible to get a speeding ticket on the Southeast Expressway because the posted speed limit of 50 m.p.h. can rarely, if ever, be attained.

In the twenty year history of the Southeast Expressway, Democratic and Republican administrations alike have neglected to provide for its maintenance. The downtown section is notorious for "breaking in" new cars. Should your car survive the pot-holes, your next problem will be to find your exit. You may get the distinct impression that Its Highness the Southeast Expressway doesn't wish you to leave it. Most exits have little or no warning; others are so inadequately marked that you may not recognize your exit when you see its sign, and you continue blithely onward. It's a safe bet, however, that it's time to turn back when you see signs for Plymouth.

We do not recommend that the average Boston Driver travel this road, but we recognize that some motorists must do so out of necessity. For these occasions there are three things no driver should be without: (1) a newspaper to while away idle moments in traffic, (2) a spare set of heavy duty shocks, and (3) a gas mask.

Storrow Drive

Running south and west from Leverett Circle along the Charles River, Storrow Drive is a major cross-town expressway. This road is appreciated by Boston Drivers for its quick access to downtown locations. In spite of its widespread use, Storrow Drive very seldom backs up severely. This does not mean that the road is without its faults. Potholes are such fixtures that many Boston Drivers know them by name. Because of the importance of Storrow Drive as a commuter road there is little likelihood they will ever be fixed. Even if they were, the relentless battering of rubber on road would ensure permanent scars in the pavement.

Out-of-state drivers who have the misfortune of attempting Storrow Drive inevitably have trouble with the placement of exit and entrance ramps. For example, the entrance from Mass. Ave. to Storrow Drive deposits the motorist onto the fast lane with no visibility of traffic coming from the other side of the hill. In addition, numerous left exits with little or no warning on the outbound side require a thorough knowledge of the layout of Storrow Drive before it can be effectively utilized by the Boston Driver.

Another hazard, usually occurring only in summer, is a concert on the Esplanade. At these times

Storrow Drive is likely to become a parking lot. Boston Drivers seem to have no qualms whatsoever about parking their cars in the outbound lanes of Storrow Drive. Free rock concerts and fireworks displays have been known to attract upwards of 200,000 people, many of whom take advantage of the free parking on Storrow Drive.

The newcomer to Boston Driving might be intrigued by the numerous signs on Storrow Drive that give the road clearance height. In spite of all the signs, a truck will periodically get wedged under a bridge because of the low clearance. If not for the fact that traffic then backs up for several miles behind the accident, it would probably be an amusing sight. On one morning some years back, a truck carrying a load of industrial-strength scissors became stuck under a bridge in this manner. As a result, some of the cargo spilled onto the pavement. Over thirty cars got flat tires, and two of these got four flat tires. The backup lasted well into the afternoon.

Sumner and Callahan Tunnels

Two places where there is never a shortage of carbon monoxide are the Sumner and Callahan Tunnels. The tunnels provide the only direct link between downtown Boston and Logan Airport. They also provide the only link to East Boston, but nobody cares about that except the people of East Boston, Winthrop, and Revere. Even on the best of days, a trip through either of these tunnels will quickly wipe the smile off your face. Two crowded, narrow lanes in each direction assure that your trip under Boston Harbor will be lengthy and unpleasant. Worst of all, the tunnels smell like a three-week-old bologna sandwich.

On top of all this, you have to pay for the privilege: 30¢ each way, with toll booths conveniently located on the East Boston side of both tunnels. Traffic is almost always backed up at the booths; typical delays range from five minutes at lunchtime to fifty minutes at rush hour. (Proper toll booth techniques are discussed in Chapter IV, "Common Obstacles—Toll Booths.") Arriving travelers at Logan Airport are in for a surprise when

The Callahan Tunnel.

they find out that even though they are only three miles from downtown Boston, it will take them an hour and a half to get there.

In conclusion, you really haven't made it as a Boston Driver until you can claim to have run out of gas in the middle of the Sumner or Callahan Tunnel and emerged with both your life and your car intact.

Lead thyself not through the shadow of the Callahan Tunnel if thou art low on fuel.

Mystic Bridge

Officially known as the Maurice G. Tobin Bridge, the Mystic Bridge carries tens of thousands of commuters daily from the North Shore across the Mystic River into Boston. Judging from the traffic flow during rush hour, most of these commuters would be going faster if they were walking. The design of the bridge is unique in that the inbound lanes are directly *above* the outbound lanes. On a clear day, the view of the city from the uppermost level (inbound lanes) can be quite spectacular.

Because traffic across it is so heavy, the bridge is always in need of repair. Because it is constantly being repaired, traffic on the bridge is always heavy. Toll booths on each level extort the 25¢ fee, which in turn finances all the other construction-related obstructions. The payment of the toll serves to guarantee your late arrival at work. Another use of tolls is to buy paint for the bridge. One reliable way for out-of-staters to identify the Mystic Bridge is that it is constantly being painted. A series of yellow lights shining against the sickly green supports of the bridge unfortunately appears in any nighttime panorama of the city of Boston.

Mass. Pike

By far the fastest land route across the state is the Massachusetts Turnpike, usually referred to as the "Mass. Pike." The Pike forms the easternmost leg of Interstate 90, a vital transcontinental route which extends to Seattle. The Pike is the straightest and fastest way out of Boston, and it is almost never clogged with traffic. The main problem with the Pike is that it is a rich man's road. To travel the nine miles of the Extension (from Weston to South Station) costs

75¢. That's over eight cents per mile, thereby making the Mass. Pike Extension the most expensive toll road in the United States. For this reason alternate routes are frequently used, but none of these can match the speed and convenience of the Mass. Pike. Aside from the price tag, the Pike suffers from an additional hazard: an occasional long home run from Fenway Park has been known to come to rest on its inbound lanes.

Route 128

This road is the major bypass around Boston, connecting the North Shore communities with those on the South Shore. Route 128 is Boston's Beltway: if not for the Atlantic Ocean, it would completely encircle the city, never getting closer than about ten miles. Both Route 128 and the Southeast Expressway are heavily-traveled commuter roads, but here the similarity ends. While drivers on the Southeast Expressway seldom go over the speed limit, drivers on 128 seldom go under it. The Southeast Expressway goes through the heart of the city; 128 goes through the heart of the suburbs. The S.E. Expressway is loaded with potholes; 128 is well-maintained. Traffic backs up frequently on the S.E. Expressway; seldom on 128. Because of the generous number of wide lanes on 128, it is the perfect place to "let 'er out" into overdrive. One final note of caution: beware of the extremely short entrance and exit lanes on 128 north in Peabody and Danvers. There are several places in this stretch where the road turns suddenly or goes down steep hills with little warning. During the winter, these hills often turn into hockey rinks, and penalties are frequently assessed. This is the only major obstacle to speedy travel through the suburbs, however.

Jamaicaway

While traveling this road, don't ever try to pass anything bigger than a motorcycle. Narrow lanes and sharp curves banked the wrong way make the Jamaicaway a Fools' Paradise for Boston Drivers. Although it is four lanes wide, the roller coaster design makes it impossible to ride two

abreast; those who try are given the choice between a head-on collision or a sideswipe. Those who are into drunken driving, beware: many a man who has had one too many has grown weary of following this poorly-lit concrete death trap and has found himself sitting in four feet of dirty water in Jamaica Pond.

Route 1

U.S. 1 goes both north and south of Boston. It is the same Route 1 that extends from northern Maine to the Florida Keys. Formerly the only north-south road through town, it is still one of the most important. Route 1 is known for its never-ending supply of gas stations, "no-tell" motels, shopping centers, and junk food restaurants. If you are stranded on Route 1, rest assured that you are never more than a two minute walk from a gas station or a five minute walk from a restaurant.

Route 93

This is the major road to New Hampshire and Quebec Province. (Route 93 also includes the Southeast Expressway, but as far as we are concerned, they are two different concepts.) North of the city, I-93 is a typical interstate highway: secure and spacious, and therefore boring. Traffic never backs up except for the southbound merge with Route 1, just past the Mystic Bridge, where it always backs up. This is a fairly new bottleneck for Boston Drivers; as recently as 1975, I-93 did not extend south of Somerville. As a result, drivers were treated to the experience of the Msgr. McGrath Highway more often than they would have preferred.

For several months after the last few miles of this "Inner Loop" had been constructed, the state highway administration refused to open the road on the grounds that a monumental traffic jam could be expected to develop as soon as the road opened. Finally, the public began to resent having paid for that multi-million dollar white elephant and not being able to use it. So the road was opened, and Bostonians have been sitting in the monumental traffic jam ever since.

Route 2

This road traverses the entire length of Massachusetts, beginning at Boston Common and extending to the New York State border. But most Boston Drivers think of Route 2 as the eight mile stretch of high-speed divided highway between North Cambridge, near Fresh Pond, and Route 128. Except for the inevitable backup on the eastbound side during morning rush hour, Route 2 is as fast as you like it, and some like it pretty fast. But beware of those gung-ho out-of-state drivers who come barreling down the big hill on the eastbound side and discover too late that Route 2 terminates quite abruptly in a traffic circle. This situation may be more than their brakes (or yours) can handle.

All good things have their price, and Route 2 is no exception. Starting from downtown, the inexperienced driver will never be able to navigate the five miles of winding, treacherous, and usually clogged roadway that separates him from the beginning of Route 2. To get there, the motorist has basically three choices: (1) take Storrow or Memorial Drive to Fresh Pond Parkway and follow the signs (if you can); (2) take I-93 north to Route 16, then take a coffee break in Medford Square before backtracking down Route 16 to Route 2; or (3) take the Mass. Pike and forget the whole thing.

Route 2

CHAPTER THREE

Basic maneuvers

In the previous two chapters you have seen some of the necessary ingredients for being a motorist in the Boston area. You now have (or should have) a beat-up car and minimal insurance. The streets are just waiting for you to drive on them. We are now ready to discuss some of the basic offensive driving techniques you will need to survive as a motorist in this city. This chapter covers some of the most popular and useful of these.

The Cutoff

The cutoff is the most frequently used Boston Driving maneuver. It is used in merge and lane change situations where there is too much congestion to enter the traffic stream easily. When two lanes merge into one, something has to give, and it might as well not be you. In these situations, you must choose a victim, establish a positional advantage, and move far enough into the lane so that the other driver cannot pass you, i.e., the victim is cut off. It is then a simple matter to move fully into the lane, ahead of the opposing driver. This is the essence of a cutoff.

A cutoff may be done from either side. It is somewhat more effective from the right because the other driver is less likely to expect a maneuver from the right. Good acceleration and braking capabilities are a definite plus, since some power and precision are required. The cutoff is more difficult with a big car due to its lower maneuverability, but it is also more effective due to the car's intimidating bulk. The ultimate in intimidation, we suppose, is your run-of-the-mill MBTA bus. Having no scruples whatsoever, the bus drivers will not hesitate to let you know who's boss. Fighting a cutoff from a bus is like trying to find a parking space in Kenmore Square on the night of a baseball game. To add insult to injury, the

The Cutoff

1. Overtake other car. 2. Edge into other lane. 3. Take other lane. 4. Finish.

bus will generally belch a big cloud of black smoke directly at you as it accelerates away.

To execute a cutoff, you must be slightly ahead of the other driver or you will not be able to edge into his lane. There must be enough clearance between your victim and the car in front of him for you to force your front end into his lane; a car-length is usually sufficient.

The possible defenses against the cutoff follow from the previous points. Ride as close as possible to the car ahead of you. With half a car-length of clearance at moderate speed, it is practically impossible to be cut off. Of course, if the car in front of you decides to brake, you both turn into hamburger, but try not to let that bother you. One way to minimize this risk is to cover the brake with your left foot. That way, you are ready either way. Avoid letting other cars overtake you, for they will then be in a position to cut you off. It might be wise to keep your options open by launching a pre-emptive cutoff strike against a driver who you suspect might be thinking about executing a cutoff against you.

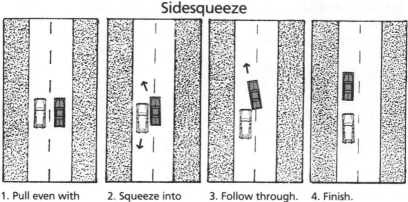

Sidesqueeze

1. Pull even with other car.
2. Squeeze into other lane.
3. Follow through.
4. Finish.

The Sidesqueeze

The sidesqueeze is similar to the cutoff, but it is done from the side of your victim rather than by moving in front. To pull off this maneuver, edge slowly closer to the opposing car. The other driver cannot afford to gamble that you really know what you are doing, so sooner or later he or she will have to brake to prevent you from colliding, in case you really have lost your marbles. When this happens, move forward as quickly as possible and take your adversary's lane when you have enough room.

You must be even with or slightly ahead of the other car; otherwise, that driver can counter by accelerating ahead of you when you try to sidesqueeze. You must also be going at about the same speed as the other car to produce the proper intimidation effect. It helps to look just a little bit unstable in driving down the road. You may be able to convince opposing drivers that you are drunk or incompetent, in which case they will almost always get out of your way and let you do anything you want.

locking

You will often be confronted with situations in which you're not sure whether you want to be in the left lane or the right lane. This can happen when you are unfamiliar with the road, or searching for an address, or perhaps looking for a parking space on either side of the street. In such situations, blocking becomes a very valuable skill.

Blocking is accomplished by straddling two lanes of traffic. The lane marker, if there is one, should split your car right down the middle. The advantages of riding between the two lanes should be obvious. No other car can get by you because there is not enough clearance on either side. And you have the flexibility to move left or right once you make up your mind which lane you want to be in. It helps to have a big car for this maneuver, since with a small car, other small cars might still be able to get by. However, you can simply side-squeeze them if they make any threatening moves.

Don't try to extend a block to three lanes: even novice Boston

Drivers can easily break up a three-lane block. Just pick a pair of adjacent lanes to block and hope for the best should you eventually need to get into the third lane. Especially if you are looking for parking, you will be going more slowly than the traffic behind you, and you are likely to be on the receiving end of horn blasts, tailgating, high

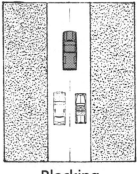

Blocking

beams, and four-letter words, as these drivers attempt to express some dissatisfaction with your behavior. It is no cause for concern, because you hold all the cards. They cannot pass by you until you let them, and there is no reason to let them intimidate you into doing so.

Intersection Techniques

Where the entire town may be the driver's battlefield, intersections are surely the "front lines". Just as battles are won and lost in the trenches, the nitty-gritty of Boston driving takes place at intersections. About half of all trip time in city driving is spent waiting at or passing through the city's intersections. Cab companies, in particular, are so riddled with intersection accidents that one company automatically assigns fault to a driver involved in one of these. So watch out! All it takes is one little bit of bad timing for a can't miss introduction to a fellow motorist.

Lights

Many years ago, local authorities decided to regulate traffic flow by placing alternating colored lamps at troublesome corners. Since for every action there is a corresponding reaction, motorists in Boston have nobly responded to the traffic signal with every conceivable ploy, all of which may be summarized by the phrase: "Paint the town green".

If the light is green, obviously you go. And quickly too, before the light changes. But suppose you have been waiting at a red light which suddenly becomes green. Do you gas it forward now? Not in this town you don't, unless you are in a chrome-eating mood. To be sure, your green light means a red light for the cross traffic, but red lights do not stop most Boston Drivers, at least not right away. We feel that a count of one one thousand, two one thousand, three one thousand should be sufficient to allow you to proceed safely.

The alert Boston Driver will condition himself to react automatically to the yellow light. The yellow follows the green, lasting several seconds before giving way to the red. This signal tells you that your green time is almost up and that you should speed up if possible, else you will be caught waiting through another light cycle. Missing a light by a second or two may prove more costly than you think, as they are often "synched". Failing to keep in one set of greens could leave you back at Kenmore Square while the alert motorist finds himself halfway to Cleveland Circle. It is worth pointing out that regardless of the circumstances, if the car in front of you foolishly stops on yellow (no doubt an out-of-state driver), it is a good idea for you to stop as well. Similarly, if the car behind you has no intention of stopping, by all means keep right on going.

One of the cardinal rules of driving is surely "Stop on Red." However, if the light is red for more than five seconds, you can assume that it is broken. You may proceed after a quick check for cross traffic and police cruisers.

Thou shall look both ways before running a red light.

If there is no threatening cross traffic, or if you are feeling lucky, it is very helpful to know precisely when your red light will turn green so you can accelerate immediately (assuming, of course, that there are no cars to run the red light in the other direction). The best way to do this is to watch for the Yellow Cross Glow. The light from the cross street turns from green to yellow just a few seconds before your green begins. When you spot the Yellow Cross Glow, get on your mark and get set, for the green is only a moment away.

Bad traffic often makes it difficult to apply many of these tips. One specific case occurs when you have the green with nowhere to go but into the rear bumper of the car in front of you. How frustrating! Traffic is backed up right to the opposite side of the intersection. The only rational relief is to go anyway. Fill any available space in the intersection even if it leaves you sitting in the middle of it. It's either you or the other guys. If you don't move up, everyone else will, leaving you behind to sit through another red light. This maneuver is illegal, but enforcement is nonexistent. If you don't believe that, prove it to yourself some evening rush hour at Berkeley and Newbury Streets.

We must reluctantly point out that Massachusetts was one of the last states in the United States to pass legislation permitting right turn on red. As soon as the measure became law, "No Turn on Red" signs began appearing on every street corner. The reason for this was that the traffic planners thought that driving conditions were chaotic enough as they were; adding right turn on red, they felt, would only make things worse. Some of the state legislators from the Boston area were gen-uinely embarrassed that Massachusetts was so far behind the rest of the nation on this issue, especially in view of the fact that their state had normally taken the lead in traffic law innovations. To make up for this, they are now gathering support for a new law permitting straight ahead on red, and there is a chance that it will pass this year. The Association of Massachusetts Junkyards, currently the most enthusiastic supporter, confidently predicts that straight ahead on red would lead to a 50 percent increase in scrap metal sales in the first year alone.

Arrows

There are times out there when it seems you don't even need to know which way you're going. That's how many traffic arrows are winking at you: left, right, straight. These are devices which thoroughly riddle the newcomer. Arrows, like lights, come in three colors. In theory, arrows only apply to vehicles heading in the direction to which they point. Complicating matters is the fact that green arrows are often used together with ordinary red lights—right on the same traffic control device.

There is an easy way through all this confusion. If any green arrow is on, you may go in any direction you like. That's all there is to it. Any further analysis is a waste of time. Red and yellow arrows, on the other hand, are so rare that they have been labeled an endangered species. Should you come across one, let logic be your guide. Don't proceed in the direction of the red arrow, and you should emerge unscathed. If you are totally confused by rainbow-colored arrows, you always have the option of waiting for them to go away or change to green.

Basic Left Turns

Because of their unique problems, few areas of Boston driving offer more potential for creativity than left turns. Taking a left almost always means crossing the oncoming lane of traffic. At intersections cars will occasionally back up in the left lane, as only a few can make their left turn each light cycle. These are just a few examples of the problems you will encounter in the course of making left turns.

If there is no light, both lanes of cross traffic must be clear before you can take your left turn. A basic solution for this problem is the Boston Left Turn, a technique developed long ago by an Allston cab driver. First you wait for the left-to-right traffic to clear. Then edge halfway across the road until the other lane clears. If any cars come from your left while you are waiting, that is just too bad for them. Make sure the front of your car is right on the center line so that no cars on your left are tempted to pass in front of you. You won't care if they pass behind you since they will not be in your way in that case.

The Beat the Green technique is a slightly more elegant maneuver. It is used when you are first in line for a left turn at an intersection with traffic lights. When the light turns green, gun the

Boston Left Turn

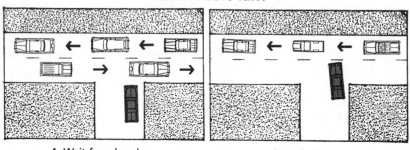

1. Wait for a break.   2. Go halfway.

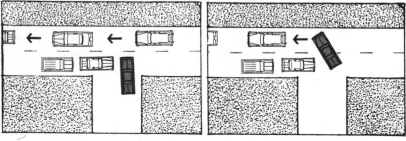

3. Wait for cross traffic.   4. Finish left turn.

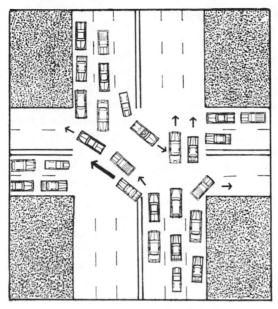

Prison Point Bridge

accelerator to make your left before the oncoming traffic catches up to you. An advanced version of this technique can be observed at the Prison Point Bridge every rush hour. When the light turns green, the first car turning left from McGrath Highway onto Cambridge Parkway invariably try to Beat the Green. The car behind him will cut to his left, effectively using car #1 as a screen. The following car does the same thing, and the process continues until there is no more space to squeeze into. Usually about four cars get through this way.

Even after all the space is gone, you may still be able to follow the "Green Beater." If the car in front of you Beats the Green, the oncoming traffic must stop. But if you tailgate the Green Beater, they will have to stop for you as well, as long as you can manage to follow so closely that oncoming cars cannot cut you off. Properly done, you will have negotiated a difficult intersection at no greater cost than an earful of horn.

Stop and Yield Signs

Stop signs bring you news which is the opposite of what you want to hear. The eight-sided red banner is an ugly sight to any Boston Driver. But take heart: it is not as bad as it seems. A full stop, though required by law, is seldom necessary. In many cases it is plain that there is no cross traffic long before the driver reaches the intersection. In others, such as the entrance to Storrow Drive off the Harvard Bridge, the intersection is so blind that there is no point in stopping at all. If you choose to make the turn just as a car comes over the hill in your lane, you will be glad that your car is fully depreciated and your life insurance is paid up. Most intersections lie somewhere in between. In general, slow down only as much as you feel is necessary to stay on top of the situation.

Four-way stop intersections are relatively uncommon in Boston. However, they are a Boston Driver's dream. Since the cross traffic must stop for their stop sign, there is no reason for you to stop also. Just take advantage of your red carpet situation.

By now it should be apparent that the triangular yellow yield signs are a waste of our nation's natural resources. A yield sign theoretically means "stop if necessary." No self-respecting Boston Driver would so much as take his foot off the gas for a yield sign. This sign, along with its cousin the flashing yellow light, are two traffic control devices which do little to control traffic.

Thou shall not yield.

Rotaries

Most visitors to Boston are surprised to find that a sign marked "Rotary" does not indicate the presence of the local Rotary Club. Rather, it forewarns the seasoned Boston Driver that he is about to enter a traffic circle. Rotaries are the epitome of anarchy and chaos on the streets of greater Boston. Seen from above, the rotary looks like a giant centrifuge, spinning cars away from its center at an amazing rate. Those legendary cows who engineered the street layout back in the seventeenth century are surely rolling over in their graves.

The Massachusetts motor vehicle code says that the cars already in the rotary have the right of way over cars entering the rotary, but don't let that fool you. The code also says that rotaries are intersections, and at an intersection, the car on the right has the right of way. Since the car on the right is always the car *entering* the rotary, it is far from clear who has the "rightest" way of all. As we have learned, the motor vehicle law has little bearing on what actually goes on anyway. In Boston's rotaries, position is everything: it depends on the configuration of the rotary whether the cars entering the rotary or already in it have the upper hand.

If the rotary is a large one, there will often be a relatively clear "speed-up" lane to the outside. It is usually easy to enter the rotary, keeping to the right as you accelerate. When up to maneuvering speed, sidesqueeze your way into the main traffic stream.

A very reliable way to enter a rotary in heavy traffic is to use a screen. This can be done if at least two lanes of traffic feed into the rotary. Get into the right feeder lane and concentrate on the car to your left; don't worry

Using a Screen

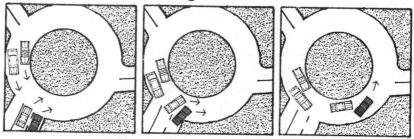

1. Start.

2. Move right when adversary moves.

3. Cut him off if desired.

about the traffic already in the circle. When your left hand opponent enters the rotary, follow him alongside to his right, thereby using him as a shield against the traffic already in the rotary. Once you are in, you will be in excellent position to cut him off, or you can just continue to his right if it suits your purposes.

Once inside the rotary, you will find that the only rule is that there are no rules. There is no protocol for lanes or lane changes because there are no lanes. A good rule of thumb is to keep to the middle, especially if you are unsure where to get off the rotary. If you keep too far left, you will find it difficult to exit; if you keep right you will get murdered by the crossfire of cars entering and exiting the

rotary. On the right you are also a sitting duck for being cut off. Keep in mind that since there are no lanes, a fine opportunity exists to practice several of the basic maneuvers described in this chapter. Just remember to look for any daylight between cars.

One word of caution is in order, however. Don't get so wrapped up in your positional struggle that you forget to exit. While it can be quite entertaining to spend an afternoon orbiting around a rotary, it isn't meant to be that way.

Weaving

Weaving is the only possible way to move through a heavy traffic stream faster than the flow. While it is most easily done on the highway at high speed, weaving is possible even in stop-and-go traffic, on any road with two or more lanes in each direction. Weaving is an excellent Boston Driving exercise because it requires execution of many of the basic maneuvers described in this chapter.

You must be going at least 10 m.p.h. faster than everybody else to be considered doing good weaving. You execute a series of cutoffs and side-squeezes. You will have to pass cars on both your left and your right as you move along. As in the case of the rotary, go for the clear lane and take on the passing problem one car at a time.

As traffic becomes heavier, weaving becomes more and more difficult because the required passing space becomes harder and harder to come by. In this situation, cars will often be riding side by side at high speed, and strategy is necessary to break them apart so you can pass them. The easiest way to solve this problem is simply to wait for a break, since two cars seldom go at the same speed for long. Pull behind the pair and block out other traffic. When one car starts edging ahead of the other, pull behind the faster car and start tailgating: this should speed him up. If not, apply pressure by turning on your high beams and blowing your horn. When you are even with the slower car, sidesqueeze him and proceed at full speed to pass the faster car. This technique often works even when the two cars are going at the same speed. In general, the larger of the two cars in tandem will be more apt to respond to the type of harassment described above. Cadillacs, in particular are pushovers.

Beat the Guillotine

Another common maneuver is known as "Beat the Guillotine." In this case, there is a slow car and a faster car ahead of you. The faster car is overtaking the slower, but the faster car isn't going all that fast. Your job is to pass the faster car and cut him off to put you in position to whiz by the slower car. But if your timing isn't very good, the faster car can be so close to the slower that you have no room for a cutoff. In this case your choice is either to give up and pull back, or proceed with the cutoff and risk being guillotined.

Beat-the-Guillotine Technique

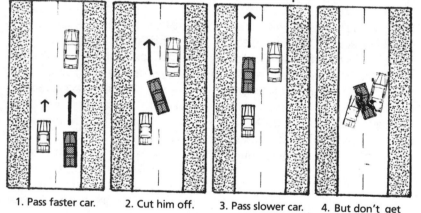

1. Pass faster car.   2. Cut him off.   3. Pass slower car.   4. But don't get guillotined!

Tailgating

If you can read the newspaper sitting in the back window of the car in front of you, you are tailgating. The driving school rule of maintaining one carlength spacing for each 10 miles per hour of speed does not apply. Boston Drivers routinely maintain a one to three carlength separation in 60 m.p.h. heavy traffic highway driving; besides, safety considerations have no bearing on the behavior of a skilled Boston Driver.

Although tailgating can be used for harassment purposes, this is not one of its primary uses. The major advantage of tailgating is that you cannot be cut off. This is important in heavy traffic or if you are trying to follow someone. Tailgating can be used to communicate to the other driver that his speed is not up to snuff, and to pressure him to either accelerate or yield to you. It can also be useful in jockeying for position during weaving situations.

The disadvantages are numerous, however. Tailgaters can still be sidesqueezed. In addition, once you are tailgating, you are not in a position to pass if such an opportunity should arise. If the car in front of you slows down, you must slow down, and at slower speed you will have more difficulty changing lanes. All in all, tailgating should be executed only when necessary, for it is a difficult Boston Driving technique of limited usefulness. Blocking is often a much more effective technique for preventing cutoffs.

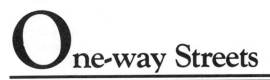

One-way Streets

Sooner or later, someone will give you some directions telling you to turn down a one-way street the wrong way. "Don't worry," you are told. "Everyone does it." And everyone *does* do it. Although one-way-the-wrong-way presents certain hazards, it is a valuable tool, because it is often the fastest way to get there, and sometimes the only way.

Occasionally, another car will have the audacity to come down the street the right way, and this might cramp your style, since most one-way streets are only one lane. If you are unable to convince him that the one-way sign has been turned around, you will have to pull over to the side into a parking space or next to a hydrant or driveway and wait for the other car to go by.

Unless you are a real daredevil, it is probably a bit too big a challenge to go down Berkeley Street or Tremont Street the wrong way (especially Berkeley, since Boston Police headquarters is on that street). One final point: a foolproof way of negotiating a one-way street the wrong way is to go in reverse. That way, you're not going the wrong way at all.

U-Turns

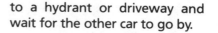

Due to mistakes in navigating, it is often necessary to make a U-turn. The first thing to remember is that "No U-Turn" signs have all the validity of a three dollar bill. They were put there to discourage Cadillac owners from tying up traffic for half an hour while they taxi their massive hulks back and forth ten times before finishing. For the seasoned Boston Driver, U-turns anywhere, anytime, present few problems.

On a residential street with little or no traffic, just make the standard three-point turn. Make sure there is not enough clearance between you and the parked cars on the other side that a passing car might try to get by.

On a busy street with lots of traffic, get into the left lane. Signal a left turn; then move a half lane to the right to give yourself a little extra room. This will confuse everybody. It will also discourage anyone from trying to side-squeeze you at least until they figure out what you are up to. Try to make the turn in one quick swoop. If there is traffic in the other direction, you will be facing across the road when you stop. It helps to have a driveway or an empty side street to help you through the turn. Now all you have to do is cut someone off to get back into the traffic stream.

With less traffic, the U-turn should be done from the right lane. Signal a right turn and pull over to the curb. If necessary, use your flashers. When the traffic clears, make the U-turn. Plenty of room. You can even cross a shallow median this way.

And then, when all else fails, there's always the old reliable gas station U-turn. Take a left into a gas station or parking lot and then pull out of the other entrance to the station back onto the road. Always go over those pressure sensitive lines that signal to the attendant that a car is in the station. You might pause just long enough to make him get up, if you are so inclined. In any event, it is always fun to hear that little bell ring.

Busy Street U-turn

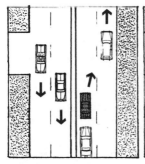 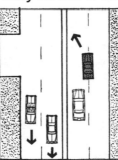 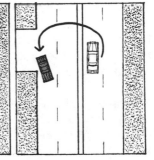

1. Get in left lane and signal left turn.

2. Move half lane to the right to get extra room.

3. Make turn in one motion, without stopping.

Bad Traffic Situations

Traffic is almost always heavy in Boston, just as it is in most major American cities. For those all too common situations where you wish you were walking, make sure you are equipped with an extensive vocabulary of four-letter words, a loud and well-turned horn, and a copy of the *Boston Globe* to pass the time in case the traffic doesn't break.

Merge Techniques

When two lanes of traffic suddenly turn into one, someone (or something) has to give. It is good Boston Driving technique to make sure neither you nor your car does the giving.

Most merge situations require a straightforward application of a cutoff or sidesqueeze. The problem is that the other driver will be trying to do the same thing. As a result, the merge becomes a game of chicken. The loser is the first one to yield. There is bluff and counter-bluff, and the game has many characteristics of a military campaign. Looking at some of those battle-scarred bumpers going in and out of the Callahan

Tunnel, you'd think there surely had been a war.

There are several things you can do to improve your chances. First, it pays to psych yourself up. Pretend you just got fired from your job. Or the Celtics just traded Larry Bird. Now look over at the other driver. It's all his fault. You can see the guilt in his eyes. You'd rather be dead than let him merge ahead of you. That's good. You're getting the idea now.

Second, it helps to have a somewhat beat-up car. If you are worried about getting a dent in your shiny new whatever, you'll choke in any merge situation, and probably get the dent as well.

Now that you have the right attitude, plunge right into the merge. Sidesqueeze your adversary as tightly as possible and move forward when you have him on the ropes. Simple, wasn't it? All it took was a little bit of properly channeled aggression. Remember to *stand your ground*. If you give an inch, you have lost the battle. The tougher Boston Driver almost always wins in a merge war because there is little opportunity for any finesse.

Fear not the merge into heavy traffic, for thine enemies will turn chicken and be vanquished.

On the Highway

Commuter expressways often have special wrong-way lanes at rush hour reserved for carpools. In theory, at least three people must be riding in the car to use this special lane. Since most cars have at most one passenger besides the driver, this lane is usually uncrowded and provides rapid transportation. There is no reason whatsoever why you need to have three people in your car to use this lane. The police could pull you over and give you a ticket, but they will never do so because the lane will be blocked if they stop you. Since this would defeat the purpose of the special lane, they have to let you get away with it. If you feel especially paranoid about it, just bring along a couple of well-dressed mannequins.

In bumper-to-bumper situations on major expressways, do not hesitate to use the breakdown lane. We do not understand why this technique is not more popular than it is. You zoom along unhindered and simply cut off whenever you want to get back into line.

Emergency Vehicles

Lady Luck has certainly smiled on you if a police car, ambulance, or fire truck comes your way while you are stuck in traffic. Most drivers pull over to the right when they see the bubble gum machine and hear the siren, but in bad traffic, there isn't room for everyone to pull over to the right, so the cars in the left lane pull to the left. This looks like the waters of the Red Sea parting. The emergency vehicle goes by, and you just pull in behind it. If you tailgate properly, you can follow it right through the traffic jam. Occasionally as many as ten cars will follow a siren this way. You must act quickly to get on the bandwagon or the Red Sea waters will close, leaving you to drown in traffic along with everybody else. This technique has the added fringe benefit of allowing you to follow the emergency vehicle through red lights, past stop signs, and down one-way streets the wrong way, as long as the location of the actual emergency is not out of your way.

Sure-fire Bumper-to-bumper Situations to Avoid.

Prevention is surely the best medicine. It is better to avoid a traffic jam entirely than to maneuver your way out of one. It pays to be aware of some specific times and places where thou shalt not drive. A few examples:

1. The Southeast Expressway during rush hour on a rainy Friday afternoon—this is where the term "heavy and slow" originated.

2. Sumner/Callahan Tunnel at rush hour—if you survive the colossal merge, you'll be asphyxiated in the tunnel.

3. Saturday afternoon downtown—the pedestrians will mow you down.

4. Memorial Drive and Harvard Square when Harvard is home for football—it's like a black hole: you get sucked in and never come out.

5. Mystic (Tobin) Bridge on Monday morning—a terrific way to add to your weekend hangover.

6. Summer Saturday mornings on Route 3 South (to Cape Cod)—don't forget your picnic lunch. Or your picnic dinner either.

7. Kenmore Square when the Red Sox are at home—if the Sox are in the pennant race, you might as well double park on Brookline Avenue and go to the game. During the 1967 season, one fan stopped his car at the entrance to the Callahan Tunnel and refused to move because Yaz was at bat in a crucial situation of a crucial game, and if he entered the tunnel his radio would go out until he reached the other side. So be prepared for anything!

CHAPTER FOUR

Common obstacles

Potholes, Pedestrians, and other Assorted Hazards

No matter how clever you are in trying to reach your destination in minimum time, you are bound to run up against many obstacles that will work against you. The alert Boston Driver should be aware of the typical road obstructions and what can be done about them.

In general, the best course of action is to avoid the obstacle entirely. Go around it, over it, or through it, if possible. Try to plan ahead so as to avoid having to come to a complete stop or being stuck in the wrong lane. If you are in a difficult position, intimidating some other driver might be a way out of your predicament. He just might let you go by, but even if he calls your bluff, at least you haven't lost anything.

The rest of this chapter will provide extensive coverage of the proper handling of some of these obstacles. You should avoid them if you can, but if you can't, this chapter will describe some techniques to minimize their impact on your Boston Driving performance.

P edestrians

Pedestrians are people who have lost their cars. They can be an awful nuisance, especially in quantity. At a busy intersection they can pile into the street in droves, allowing even an excellent Boston Driver no chance to break through the line. Even in good traffic, a pedestrian can often force a stop by simply barging into the street. The Boston Driver has his size and speed going for him, while the pedestrian has more mobility plus the right of way, the latter being not particularly useful on the streets of Boston.

Most pedestrians fall into one of three distinct types of personalities, as described below.

The *Tenderfoot* is afraid of Boston Drivers and will scan for an opening in traffic. When he finds one, he will shoot across the street at top speed. This type of person generally presents no problem. He will be long gone before you can even think about reaching him. However, Tenderfoot will occasionally misjudge the situation, giving you life or death responsibility over him. Especially if you are in a good mood, chances are you will brake and spare his life. However, to insure that this incident does not recur, particularly with you driving, you should seize the opportunity to voice your opinion of his behavior as bluntly as possible. Try jamming on the brakes (squeaky ones are a definite plus), and add a blast of horn if desired. Sometimes this will cause Tenderfoot to freeze; even if it doesn't, come as close to him as you can, open your window, and curse him briefly

but loudly enough for everyone to hear. Properly done, these procedures should result in your pedestrian victim never again hindering you or any other Boston Driver.

The *Cool Cat* acts very nonchalant when crossing the street. This type walks at a slow pace, is never in a hurry, and will never break stride for you without some show of Boston Driving on your part. He will usually stare you down as he crosses the street. For this type, stronger measures are required. Head right toward him at full speed and pull behind him at the last minute. Since he will be looking right at you all the way, it is important to swerve close to him. This technique will often persuade Cool Cat to stop or go back to the curb before he gets in your line of fire. This approach works equally well on Tenderfoot, since he will run away as fast as he can, never to return.

The third type, known as the *Snake,* also appears relaxed and unruffled by the prospect of crossing the street. However, he will have the further audacity to look straight ahead, or worse, read a newspaper as he ambles across the street. The Snake is very clever because he really

knows everything that's going on. He probably has mirrors in his newspaper. The intimidation maneuvers used for Cool Cat will still work occasionally on the Snake, but a more effective approach is to fight fire with fire. Approach the intersection with *your* head buried in a newspaper, or try carrying on a conversation with someone in the back seat. Turning your head and appearing to be oblivious to the situation is very important. If the pedestrian suspects that you are not aware of his presence, he will usually get out of your way.

At one time or another, a passenger in your car may have offered you "two points if you hit this one." These "points" are awarded explicitly for striking pedestrians. It is not necessary to injure them to obtain points, but a knockdown is required. Points have no value except as a measure of Boston Driving prowess in dealing with pedestrians. Once earned, points remain in your Boston Driving account for life; they can never be taken away. In recent years, there has been some confusion concerning point values for striking certain categories of pedestrians. We have compiled a list of target values that has been sanctioned by the Boston Association for People-Free Streets, the organization responsible for recording points and arbitrating any disputes concerning points.

Pedestrian Point Values

Typical Able-Bodied Pedestrian	3
Little Old Lady (with raised cane)	2
Little Old Couple	3
Pregnant Woman	2
Baby Carriage (empty)	1
Baby Carriage (with baby in it)	3
Bicyclists	6
Tourists	1
Dogs	½
Harvard Jock	10
Absent-Minded M.I.T. Professor	2
Policeman	8
Mayor	10
Governor	15
Anyone carrying three or more packages (for each additional package, add ½)	2
Gas Station Attendant	5
Groups of three or more people (for each additional person, add 1)	6

Trolleys and Buses

Trolleys and buses would be no more bothersome than big, slow cars if not for the fact that they stop every other second to pick up or drop off passengers. A fortunate fact of life is that trolleys must stay on the tracks, but your car is free to go anywhere on the roadway. If you are blocking a trolley by straddling the tracks, it has only one option: it must stop. You have two—you can stay in the lane on the tracks or move away. Take advantage of this situation because you are in command. Don't be intimidated by the trolley's lights, the tinkling of its bell, or four letter words from the driver, because there is nothing the trolley driver can do until you let him.

On Huntington Avenue, you will be competing with the Arborway trolleys for road space. They share the road with you, but they are restricted to the left lane, so you can block them easily. With the trolley behind you, its frequent stops for passengers are of no consequence. On Commonwealth Avenue and Beacon Street, you will occasionally need to take a left or U-turn across the tracks. If traffic is heavy enough, and you are crazy enough, just turn onto the tracks and wait. Make sure you are fully blocking the tracks so that the trolley driver has no notions of trying to get by you. If you really want to impress the subway riders, block both lanes of trolley traffic while you are waiting to turn.

The most common public transportation vehicle is the MBTA bus. As long as you avoid getting stuck behind one, their presence on the streets is tolerable. Let one in front of you, and you'll be in for a rough time. The least of your problems will be the stench of unburned diesel fuel straight from the bus's exhaust. Worse, you will have to suffer as it stops repeatedly to pick up or discharge passengers. Your progress is completely at the mercy of the bus driver if he blocks enough lanes that you do not have room to pass him even when he does stop. To add insult to injury, discharged passengers will often attempt to walk in front of you as they cross the street.

Dogs

A nice way of characterizing dogs in the Boston area is to say they are a bit short on survival instinct. A more accurate way of characterizing them is to say they are stupid. Nearly all unleashed dogs look at the streets as their personal playground and are completely oblivious to the hazards of the roads. These are, of course, the essential attributes for a good Boston Driver. If dogs could live to be seventeen years old they could get their licenses and become first-rate Boston Drivers.

Because the dog usually doesn't know what he's doing, there is no maneuver that is guaranteed to get him off the street. A large dose of horn usually turns the trick; however, in recent years many species have become resistant to this treatment. Slamming on the brakes as you pull up to the dog may intimidate him, but he is just as likely to start sniffing up the bugs caught in your radi- ator grill. If anyone out there knows a sure-fire secret of dog removal, please let us know. At the moment there is no known cure for the common dog.

Parked and Double-parked Cars

It is mighty frustrating to find yourself in the right lane behind a double-parked car, with an otherwise clear lane ahead of you and gobs of traffic whizzing by on your left. "Why me?" you ask. "What did I do to deserve this?" If you are in this situation, you are certainly going nowhere fast. Although you might have to wait for a big enough break in the traffic to switch to the left lane, corrective measures can often be taken.

If you are first in line at an intersection with a parked car in your lane on the other side, you might first try the "peace talks" approach. First, take a quick look at the driver to your left and assess his Boston driving savvy, taking into consideration the condition of his car, the expression on his face, and the probable state of his reflexes. After

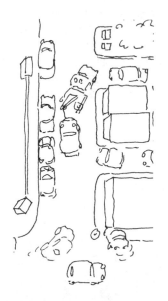

this, if you feel confident, give some kind of gesture indicating that you would like to proceed through the intersection ahead of him.

The blitz approach is usually best. Gun your accelerator as soon as the light turns green and cut off the car in the left lane. This maneuver is very similar to the "Beat the Guillotine" technique described in Chapter III. It will always work unless the other driver is exceptionally alert; even then, he will often let you go anyway just to get rid of you.

If the left lane traffic has you beaten, pull into the intersection anyway. At worst, you can go when the light turns yellow and the left lane subsequently clears. If someone slows down for a left turn, you've got it made, since he will be blocking for you. It's one of the few situations where you can shift to the left lane without even bothering to look. This also works if you are caught behind a car waiting to take a left turn.

Similar techniques apply to the problem of pulling out of a parking space into the traffic stream. In this situation don't try any maneuver until you are sure you can clear the parked car ahead of you. It can be very embarrassing to execute a neat cutoff only to find that you have left your front bumper dangling on the rear of the car parked in front of you.

Cutoff on Green Light

1. Stopped at intersection.

2. Surge forward and execute cutoff.

3. Finish.

Bicycles

Dealing with pedestrians, trolleys, dogs, and doubleparked cars is work enough for the most seasoned of Boston Drivers. But there is yet another obstacle that continues to gnaw away at valuable road space: the bicycle. Bike riders are a strange bunch. They tend to feel very self-righteous about physical fitness, saving energy, and preserving the environment, yet at the same time they fail to realize they are breathing more exhaust than anybody else. They claim they have a right to be part of the traffic stream, but the truth is they can't cut it in the Big Leagues. Sometimes, they take up enough of the road to slow down traffic significantly, and corrective measures are indicated.

Most bicycle riders, like pedestrians, exhibit one of several distinct personalities, as follows:

Mr. Safety always obeys the traffic lights, rides with his hands on the brakes at all times, always keeps to the right, and even signals turns. He is a religious fanatic, and the Motor Vehicle Code is his bible. Mr. Safety probably owns a crackerjack bicycle and the best lock money can buy. At night you can always recognize him by his phosphorescent armbands and enough reflectors to light up Copley Square. If he is coming toward you, it will feel like you're staring into a high beam.

In reality, Mr. Safety has a love-hate relationship with his bicycle. Although he derives some enjoyment from the exercise, as all bikers do, he is deathly afraid of cars. He feels inferior because your car is bigger and faster than his bike. The outcome of any showdown between his bike and a car is certain, and he knows it. Consequently, he usually suffers from chronic paranoia and expects you to try to swat him like a fly.

As a result, this species of bicyclist is beaten before he starts. The slightest sign of aggressiveness on your part will send him scurrying into the shoulder, out of sight and out of mind. Often he will be out of your way long before you reach him. Many Boston Drivers have never even been able to take a good close look at this highly elusive creature.

Lefty is a different breed of biker who likes to ride on the left side of the road. Usually he rides sitting up with one hand on the handlebars. The other hand is unpredictable: it might be doing anything on the spectrum of scratching his navel to writing his memoirs. The hand controlling the bicycle is willing to lend itself if necessary to the more executive work being done by the other hand. This leaves nothing steering the bike, but it always seems to keep going anyway.

Lefty is intrigued by the thought of watching his own death unfold before him. Riding on the left, he will have full view of the car that hits him. If he were to ride on the right, he would likely get hit from behind and would thereby be denied the cosmic experience of watching himself be killed. Of course, by riding on the left, he increases the chances of the Big Event significantly, but this is no deterrent.

Lefty is more of a hazard to other bicycle riders and pedestrians than he is to cars, but he is still a damn nuisance. Lefty thinks all Boston Drivers are aggressive and malicious toward bicycles (he's right), but he also thinks he is so much smarter he can react to any dangerous situation that could develop.

The best place for a bicycle.

Of course he is wrong, and it is easy to defend your turf as a motorist against any bicycle encroachment. When you see Lefty coming at you, just pull to the right slightly and coax him gently off the road. After a few incidents like this, Lefty may be convinced that continuing in this manner could be hazardous to his health. As a general policy, we advocate putting bicyclists in their place: either walking their bikes on the sidewalk or riding them on bike paths, as far as possible from the world of Boston Driving.

A third type of bicycle rider, known as *Aggressor,* is always racing against the traffic. He usually loses, but that doesn't bother him. As a general rule, he will keep to the far right if he cannot keep up with the cars; at the same speed as the traffic, he will move left to take up a full lane. Given the opportunity, he will pass cars and buses on the left or right, block when it suits him, and weave in and out of traffic. At a light, he will weave to the front of the line, give a quick glance for cross traffic, and run the light, barely missing a stride. This species of bicyclist pushes his maneuverability advantage to the hilt. Most ride hands on brakes and can stop on a dime. Aggressor is seldom afraid to cut off a car.

If you run into one of these personalities, be aware that you are up against a tough competitor. They are just about impossible to maneuver into a situation where you can threaten to squeeze them to death between lanes of traffic or between traffic and parked cars. If one blocks your lane, the best thing to do is to try to sidesqueeze him to the middle of the traffic stream. This will force the bicyclist to weave and will usually occupy him enough to allow you to pass him. But beware: if he's good, he will move with you and prevent you from doing so.

Potholes

One of the first signs of spring in Boston is the big clunk you hear and feel when driving over a pothole. Potholes may be characterized as small pieces of roadway that aren't there. They are consequences of those fine New England winters. The relative warmth of a late winter's day melts the snow and ice on the road, and the water seeps into the pores of the pavement. At night, the water freezes and expands, exerting pressure on the road surface and weakening it. The resulting faults in the surface grow bigger and bigger with each passing car until, if nothing is done, a good-sized crater appears on the road surface. There are other sources as well. Many a pothole owes its creation to a hungry snowplow. It is said that Boston has a unique type of plow that scoops up the asphalt while leaving the snow behind.

Most potholes are formed from about mid-February to mid-March. By April Fools' Day the snow has melted, and with it has gone the excess water necessary to form potholes. At this time, the city sends out its maintenance crews to fix some of them. They always run out of money before the job is done, so it's a safe bet that if a particular pothole is still around on Mother's Day it will be there until next spring. Even the chasms that are repaired always have a slight bump where the new asphalt was added. After a few hundred repairs have been made to a stretch of road, it begins to feel like a bed of rocks when you drive on it. Only a complete resurfacing can restore sanity at this point; however, the budget for this type of repair is so small that it takes years before money can be appropriated, and another year or so to do the job.

Steer clear of potholes, for they are the portals of hell.

Where to find potholes:

Due to the spotty record of the road crews in repairing potholes, it can be quite difficult to predict where you will encounter your next one. Every winter affects each street differently; however, there are a few types of streets that tend to get more than their fair share:

1. *Heavy Traffic Streets.* Potholes can spring up any time on the major streets of Boston and the surrounding suburbs. The constant pounding of bus and truck tires imposes tremendous stress on the road surface, and the slightest little crack in the pavement quickly turns into a voluminous crater. Some potholes are so deep that a car can fall in up to its axle and have to be towed out. It pays to remember where these are located since it can be quite a while before they are repaired.

2. *Industrial Areas.* Again, large trucks take their toll. Since there is little passenger car traffic on these streets, they are allowed to deteriorate to a much worse condition than the more heavily trafficked arteries. While it might seem like a shortcut to sneak by the warehouses of Andrew Square instead of going through typical rush hour traffic, it isn't worth it when you consider that you'll probably need a new set of shock absorbers by the time you finish.

3. *Bridges.* Since their roadways are not supported by Mother Earth, bridges are notoriously vulnerable to pothole formation. As any bicyclist will tell you, it is wise to be aware of these bridge potholes ahead of time, or you run the risk of making a big splash.

4. *Residential Streets.* Although they often don't get too much traffic, residential streets are prime candidates for potholes since they are usually paved with a thinner, lower quality grade of asphalt. Although they don't tend to get very deep, they do tend to stick around for a long time because the lack of heavy traffic gives them a lower priority for resurfacing. Some resourceful folks we know in Belmont are raising a fine crop of tomatoes on what used to be part of their street.

The "Warp-5" Approach

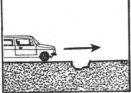  

1. Speed up toward pothole.

2. Remain airborne over pothole.

3. Don't leave anything behind.

How to Avoid Potholes:

1. *Swerve Technique.* If the pothole is seen well in advance, simply change lanes. If someone is already there, side-squeeze him. Block if you can, to give yourself the flexibility to swerve to either side.

2. *Straddle Approach.* In this maneuver, the pothole passes harmlessly under the car, between the wheels. This method has the advantage that it is usually not necessary to divide your attention between missing the pothole and cutting someone off. But it requires planning and precise maneuvering to avoid hitting the pothole, especially if it is wider than your front axle.

3. *The "Warp-5" Approach.* If you see the pothole too late and you must go over it, accelerate to the maximum speed possible before hitting the pothole. The theory is that the wheels will "float" over the pothole with minimal damage. The problem with this theory is that unlike the average pothole, it does not hold water. On a bad day, you could lose your front end, transmission, or both. Subscribers on this theory have been seeing too many Burt Reynolds movies.

4. *The "Easy-does-it" Approach.* In this maneuver, the pothole is once again seen too late to avoid. Slow to the minimum speed possible on the theory that the lower your speed, the less the damage. The problem here is that you can sometimes get stuck if the pothole is big enough and you are going too slowly. Prayer upon crossing the threshold is recommended.

Toll Booths

Toll booths are found on only three major arteries in the Boston area: the Mystic Bridge, the Sumner/Callahan Tunnels, and the Mass. Pike. A toll booth is the only obstacle that doesn't just slow you down: it detains you until you submit to its blackmail. Unfortunately, the outlook for cash-free alternatives is bleak. The shortest non-toll alternative from downtown to the airport is at least forty-five minutes longer than the Callahan Tunnel. Similarly, Route 99, with its zillions of traffic lights, is a poor substitute for the Mystic Bridge. And Route 9 is no match for the Mass. Pike.

So face it: you're going to have to pay. If you're feeling particularly stingy and are thinking about running it, bear in mind that you are really playing a low stakes game of Russian Roulette. You will get away with it most of the time, but your number will come up sooner or later. Your only choice is whether to drive through the attended toll booth or settle up in the Exact Change Lane (E.C.L.).

If you go the E.C.L. route, you are expected to toss your money into the big funnel (no pennies, please) and wait for the signal to turn from red to green. The green light always has a big "THANK YOU" written across its face, even though there was just a hint of coercion. If you do go into the E.C.L., be sure you have the E.C. Many drivers were last seen by human eyes as they were fumbling through their pockets, glove compartment, and under the seat in a vain attempt to find E.C. for the E.C.L.

A less serious error is to miss the hopper when you toss your coin. If this happens, three choices are open to you: 1) toss another coin; 2) get out of your car, find the coin, and slam-dunk it back into the hopper; or 3) run the booth. Our recommendation would be to run it. If you are stopped, advise the officer that the machine is obviously malfunctioning. And stick with your story, no matter how bad a liar you are. After all, you have paid. The disadvantage of tossing an additional coin is obvious:

you will have paid twice. This option should be reserved for absolute panic situations, or if you have already been caught twice previously that day.

Coin tossing in E.C.L.'s is something of a sport within the sport of Boston Driving. Many techniques exist to solve the problem of moving the coin from the driver's hand into the toll basket. A driver can bank shot or stuff it with either hand, but it is easier with the left hand. A leading, high-arc toss is ideal for the left-hander who is late for an appointment. For the hopelessly right-handed, we recommend the "around-the-world" hook shot by the passenger through his side window and back over the roof of the car. A simpler, but less elegant technique for righties is an across-the-body backhand flip shot. For those cars equipped with sunroofs, tossing techniques are almost limitless. A little experimentation with the various options will soon make it clear which is the best technique for you.

An advanced technique is to toss your coin and drive through the booth before the light turns green and has a chance to thank you. To pull this off, you must approach the booth with your coin in your left hand and your window open. Toss your coin a few feet in front of the basket, continuing through the booth at a steady speed of at least 10 m.p.h. The expert will aim his coin for the far side of the basket because a direct hit is likely to turn the green light on too quickly. Hitting the far side of the basket will insure enough time for the driver to get through the booth before the light turns green. Of course, an even slightly errant toss will sail over the basket completely. So it's not as easy as it sounds. A 50 percent success rate is considered excellent.

The rules are somewhat different for attended toll booths. The presence of a human being offers diverse possibilities for personality interaction. You might simply hand over your money with an icy stare, or you might have a brief but pleasant discussion on this year's prospects for the Red Sox, or perhaps on the perennial corruption in the state house. But whatever you do, don't ask the toll taker for directions. They speak very rapidly in an attempt to get rid of you and thereby keep the line moving. This combined with the inevitably thick Boston accent, makes it almost impossible to understand them. But even if you do catch every word, you can be sure that every word is wrong. People who rely on directions from toll collectors usually end up lost at the Charlestown dump, and many have never returned to civilization. A toll taker on the Mystic Bridge told us that he gives the same set of directions to all inquiries: "Across the bridge to Storrow Drive, second exit, around the circle, and you're there."

A couple of other points are worth mentioning. The E.C.L.'s tend to be more popular with motorists than the attended booths; consequently, in heavy traffic the attended booths are sometimes faster, even though you might have exact change. If you do have correct change, and choose to pay at the manned booth, remember that it is considered poor etiquette to leave the toll plaza with any part of the collector's arm in your possession.

Trucks

Doing battle with a truck is like taking on the front four of the Pittsburgh Steelers: if you're lucky, you'll bounce off. On a bad day, they can turn into a pancake. In spite of bumper stickers which say, "Drive safely," trucks are the only vehicles that will never consider yielding. Why should they? Their survival is never in doubt. You don't need to see a truck to know that it is coming. Ill-mannered, loud, and foul-smelling, trucks always give ample warning of their presence. However, there is no need to panic at the first sound of the diesel monster. The Boston Driver has two key assets at his disposal: speed and maneuverability. Like the English Navy that outfoxed the Spanish Armada, the good Boston Driver will easily be able to reduce any truck to a minor nuisance.

Trucks would present little obstacle if not for the truck drivers. Truck drivers are usually men with above average height and weight and look like they haven't seen a shower in a week. Many carry a sticker on the back of their trucks proclaiming: "This vehicle paid $662,523,987.50 [or some other equally ridiculous amount] in road use taxes last year." That, they believe, entitles them to behave as if they own the road. Also, since their vehicles are bigger than anyone else's, they will often drive as if no one else is around. One sticker you probably won't see is one announcing that the truck's owner has paid a like amount in fines for exceeding load limits and other violations of federal and state law.

The mere presence of a truck should not cause you to run and hide. Almost any heavy truck can be passed on an uphill grade. If a truck is riding directly behind you and breathing down your neck, a speed-up is the easiest solution. You could slow down to harass him, but this is an unnecessary risk.

Because of their size, trucks should never be taken lightly, and there are a number of pitfalls to beware. If you are tailgating a truck in wet weather, be sure to keep your windshield wipers on, or else be prepared to

be blinded and buried under an avalanche of water and mud. If the truck is carrying open cargo, be prepared for an unscheduled delivery directly in front of your car at any moment. Depending on what kind of cargo is being carried, you will have to be prepared to react. Another especially bad time to be in back of a truck is at a toll booth. Despite the $662,523,987.50 paid in road use taxes, it never fails to take forever for the truck driver and the toll attendant to settle up.

When it finally does leave the booth, be wary of falling asleep waiting for the truck to accelerate up to speed. Finally, don't ever let yourself get caught between a truck and the guard rail, for you might end up instantly transformed into a sausage pizza.

The most important advice is not to let the truck driver intimidate you. Just remember to keep your cool, and leave that mothertrucker behind.

CHAPTER FIVE

Parking

Whatever your destination, you will eventually have to park your car. It would be so nice to be able to step out of the car, push a button, and watch the car collapse to the size of a pack of cigarettes. Unfortunately, life is not so easy, and if you're trying to park in front of North Station on the night of a Stanley Cup playoff game, life can be downright difficult. Even though you cannot fold up your car in George Jensen style, do not despair. Parking in Boston is a challenge that nourishes the creative mind like no other. There are lots of opportunities for the skilled Boston Driver to demonstrate his prowess in the quest for a parking space. Although parking is often an annoying hassle, we believe that no one should ever have to avoid driving for fear of not being able to find a free parking space.

Tickets, Tows, and Denver Boots

Every driver is happy to find a legal parking space in a congested area. But many Boston Drivers are unaware of the extra opportunities that illegal parking offers. You can count on lots of spaces to choose from, and you can usually get close to your destination. However, there are certain pitfalls to beware. Although none of these are likely, you can get a ticket. Or towed. Or the worst of all possible fates: the Denver Boot, alias "The Immobilizer."

Tickets range in severity from two dollars for overnight parking in the suburbs to twenty dollars or more for rush hour parking on a busy downtown street. The best course of action when you get a ticket is to throw it away. At worst, it will be several months before the authorities come after you.

Some Boston Drivers, rather than throw them away, proudly display their ticket collections. These are usually stacked neatly in the glove compartment and can be produced on request at a moment's notice. Others let them dangle from the rear-view mirror, shuffling in the vent exhaust. The only legitimate use of tickets that we know of is to leave them under your windshield wiper in order to discourage meter maids. By never touching the ticket, you have not even acknowledged its presence.

If you happen to become one of the unlucky few to be pursued by the authorities, the next step will be for you to receive a nasty notice in the mail increasing your fine by some small amount, say $5, though in practice they'll still accept the original fine and consider themselves lucky to get it. After several more months, they will send an even nastier notice, threatening to take away firstborns or some other equally horrible fate. If you still don't pay, the Department of Motor Vehicles may refuse to renew your license or registration until you make your peace with them. Before letting things get to this

state, you should consider re-registering your car in order to get new tag numbers, especially if you have run up a big tab with the meter maids. This will set the bad guys months behind in tracking you down and punishing your criminal behavior.

Getting towed is less of a joke. The police will sometimes tow you if you park illegally on a public street. However, most towing is done by private companies whose "clients" are businesses with parking lots. The business makes a deal with the towing company to tow everybody parking in the lot at certain hours (usually overnight). The tow costs you, the vehicle owner, $24, a rate regulated by the city and far exceeding the towing company's cost of kidnapping your car. The $24 must be paid in cash. No checks please, for you might stop payment. And the companies are not yet progressive enough to take Master Charge. Let's face it: your car is being held for ransom. The excess profits are spent on such things as attack dogs, barbed wire fences, and other security measures designed to prevent you from stealing back your own car.

This is your

BOOT REMOVAL KIT

License Plate no._____

Is an Illegal Space Right for You?

The alert Boston Driver should bear in mind that there is always a chance of being "caught" when parking illegally. The chances of being caught and the likely consequences should always be taken into consideration. Here are some important questions to ask yourself:

1. *Is it a tow zone?* The likelihood of being towed is an important factor. You should favor spaces which do not impede traffic flow. Some places to avoid are the entrance to the Mass. General Hospital Emergency Room, the center lane of the Central Artery, and the Governor's space in the statehouse parking lot.

2. *Are other cars parked nearby?* Parking in a tow zone is a much better risk if there are lots of other cars parked there as well. Being towed is unlikely because the police would have to do the same to everyone else parked in the tow zone. Furthermore, many of the other cars are probably owned by neighborhood residents who know that the area is safe. At worst you will get a ticket, but it is usually worth the risk. On the other hand, if you would be the only car in the no parking zone, beware, for you are begging for the jaws of the tow truck.

3. *How long will you be parked?* For a minute, almost anything goes; for a week, better keep your nose clean. We know of one friend who claims to have double-parked in front of Jordan Marsh all day one Saturday (before Washington Street was closed to traffic), but even we find this hard to believe.

4. *How much of a hassle is walking?* If it is pouring rain, or ten below zero, or you are carrying some packages, you will want to get as close as you can. In this case, you would want to pass up a legal space far away from your destination if you can find an illegal one further up that better meets your needs.

Cruise Techniques

Let's say you are riding down the street looking for a parking space. This is known as cruising. The first rule to remember is to cruise as close as possible to the middle of the street, blocking if necessary, in order to give yourself the flexibility to grab a space on either side. When you see a space on the right, proper procedure is to put on your right blinker, pull over just past the space, and go into reverse. This claims the space for you. If anyone has the audacity to front into the space while you are getting ready to back into it, you should calmly get out of your car and ask the other driver to leave, for he has committed a serious breach of parking space ethics. If he refuses, you are then justified in coming back in fifteen minutes and letting the air out of his tires, or worse. Fortunately, this type of impropriety is fairly infrequent.

The real challenge in a cruise situation is to grab a space on the

Parking "by ear."

Proper fire hydrant parking technique.

left side of a two-way street. The best approach is to have someone in your car stand in the space until you get there. U-turns into a parking space are very hard to execute properly. If you go around the block in order to face the proper direction, the space will usually be gone.

Thou shall grab the first parking place thou seest, for a second chance will never come to thee.

Do not overlook the possibilities of "quasi-legal" spaces while cruising. Street corners, taxi stands, and crosswalks are technically illegal, but one rarely gets a ticket, much less towed, so these spaces are as good as legal ones. Fire hydrants present another good source of parking spaces. Theoretically, there must be at least ten feet clear on either side of a fire hydrant; in practice, one firehose-width is sufficient. Actually, the best way to handle hydrants is to bring along an empty garbage can, place it upside down over the hydrant, and put the cover on top. Nobody, especially the police, will be the wiser. In residential areas, you may be able to "borrow" a garbage can if you don't already have one along. What to do with the trash that may already be in it is an interesting problem for which we do not have a ready solution.

[83]

Street Cleaning

Parking is banned on some streets for two to four hours each week, allegedly for street cleaning. Most of the time, the street cleaning is not done and no cars are towed. No doubt this does little to improve Boston's reputation as a filthy city. Sometimes the street cleaning is done around the parked cars. Once in a *great* while, *everybody* parked in the street cleaning zone will be towed. By the time the street is clear of cars, the two hours are up, parking is legal again, and the street cannot be cleaned. This is the ultimate joke of Boston street cleaning: they can tow you and they don't even have to disturb the slime on the street. Evidently, it is easier to remove thousands of pounds of automobiles than a few measly pounds of dirt.

If you do park in a street cleaning zone, however, you will get away with it almost every time. If possible, park in the middle of the zone; then glance over about ten minutes after the ban goes into effect. If you see tow trucks, you will probably have time to rescue your car before it is kidnapped. If not, congratulations; you are safe for the entire duration of the street cleaning period.

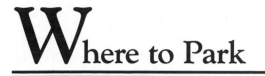

Where to Park

Downtown shopping area

Take the subway. During shopping hours there is absolutely no hope, and you may be stuck in traffic. If you are willing to walk across the Common, you can almost always find a space in nearby Beacon Hill, and sometimes it will even be legal.

South Station area

During business hours it is very tough, but Chinatown is always worth a try. If you are picking someone up at the railroad station, just park in front, throw your flashers on, and go inside. Flashers are always good for fifteen minute parking—anywhere, anytime. Nights and weekends, legal street parking is easy to find near the railroad station.

Government Center/ Haymarket/North Station

With the development of Faneuil Hall, finding prime parking spots in this part of town has become a big challenge. You can often find a space under the Central Artery overpass on Surface Road. Most of the spaces have meters, but don't fret if you don't have the right change. Considering all the out-of-state cars that converge on this part of town, the police have pretty much given up on parking enforcement in the area. After dark, there's never a problem anyway since the meters are not in effect. Another trick you might try is to check the streets between North Station and Haymarket, on Haverhill, Canal, Friend, or Portland Streets, southeast of Causeway Street.

For North Station, parts of Nashua and Lowell Streets are accessible only from Leverett Circle, and parking is plentiful. It is also illegal, but we have never heard of a ticket being given here. Even on the night of a Boston Garden event, these spaces do not fill up until about fifteen to thirty minutes before game time.

Back Bay

Primarily a residential area, Back Bay is not too tough to crack during the day, when the residents are at work. Newbury and Boylston Streets are difficult all the time, however. Marlborough and Beacon Streets have never failed to produce a parking space, but they are the furthest from the Boylston Street stores. If you value neither your car nor your life, you can slipslide through the rows of stripped cars and mugging victims and park on Back Street. Should your car survive the thieves who hang out there, it will probably be towed. Parking on Back Street is illegal and enforced.

Theater District

A space can always be found in Bay Village, a small residential area bounded by Stuart, Arlington, and Tremont Streets. The houses look very similar to those of Beacon Hill, and the area seems seedy at first glance. However, rumor has it that the area is, in fact, quite safe, and we are unaware of any pattern of North End style vandalism in this part of town. In any case, parking in this area is illegal, but there is no enforcement.

Kenmore Square

Beacon Street as far as Mass. Ave. usually yields something, and Bay State Road is always worth the gamble. You can always park at a street corner, hanging over the curb a little bit, but be careful: lots of tickets are given out at Kenmore Square.

If it's the night of a baseball

game, you can get away with almost anything. People have been known to double-park on Brookline Avenue. We don't recommend this because even if you don't get towed, you will have a terrible time getting through the hordes of pedestrians that pour into the streets after the game. You might try parking on the Brookline side of Park Circle; it's a fifteen minute walk, but on a nice summer evening, who cares? After the game is over, you must *head away* from Kenmore Square, even if it means going out of your way. If you don't, you run the risk of sitting in the black hole of postgame cars and pedestrians for quite a while longer than you bargained for.

Brookline Avenue/ Hospitals

First try should be the streets between Brookline Avenue and the Riverway. If these don't work you can always cross the subway tracks and park on Chapel Street. It's only a five minute walk from there to the hospitals, but remember: no overnight parking in Brookline.

Harvard Square

Most Boston Drivers think this is the toughest park of all. The first thing to try is the set of legal spaces on Eliot Street before it runs into Boylston Street. These usually fill by 9 A.M., and you will be exceptionally lucky to find one after that time. Should you score one, they are fine for overnights, as long as your car is too shabby to steal. For short-term parking, the numerous metered spaces around Harvard Square are fine. Enforcement is spotty, but at a cost of 20¢ per hour, it hardly seems worth it to be a lawbreaker.

A number of office buildings in the Harvard Square area have private parking lots. As long as you don't block anybody or park there during business hours, these are fine. They all have a warning you will be towed, but it is a bluff, because at off hours, there is no one around to call the towing company.

For lots with attendants, one trick which has always been successful for us is to pull into the lot as if you own it. Wave at the attendant if there is one and don't look back. It helps to be well-dressed and look official. Chances are, the attendant will be too engrossed in his game of solitare to even notice you, much less care.

Convenient sidewalk parking

Try Winthrop Street, west of Boylston. The street is extremely narrow, but if you can get your car onto the sidewalk, nobody will bother you.

Residential streets near the Square are an unreliable last resort. Between Brattle and Mt. Auburn Streets are several cross streets with potential parking, but you are likely to walk a long way even if you find a space. The same problem applies to all streets east of the Mass. Ave./Mt. Auburn Street intersection near Orson Welles Cinema.

Allston/Brighton

Stop anywhere. Shut off the motor. Lock up. Voila: a safe parking space.

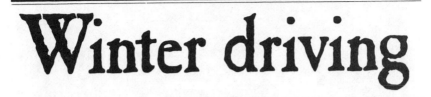

CHAPTER SIX

Winter driving

New England winters do not have the greatest of reputations; in fact, they are downright depressing. Proper Bostonians complain almost as much about the wind, cold, snow, and ice as they do about the Mystic Bridge on Monday morning. Winter driving applies to only a few months each year, but it is worth being prepared for the additional hazards and opportunities.

Snow Emergencies

Let's say it is January, and we have just been hit by a nice fourteen-inch Northeast'er. Now what happens? Well, that depends. If conditions are rotten enough, the mayor will declare a snow emergency. This means that parking is prohibited on certain designated streets in the metropolitan area. At all other times, parking on these streets is perfectly legitimate. Generally, the beginning and end of a snow emergency is announced on all the radio stations. It remains in effect until the city has had a chance to do as much plowing as it feels like doing and calls it off.

"Snow emergency" is a form of martial law. Boston Drivers have no rights and may be treated very arbitrarily without appeal. The behavior of the authorities is erratic in snow emergency situations. Most of the time, they will plow around you if you leave your car parked on a snow emergency street, leaving you with a big shoveling job to get your car but not any other inconvenience. Occasionally the plows will deliberately bury your car with all the excess snow on the street. You will have to shovel the equivalent of a driveway full of snow to free your car. In this case you will have so much to shovel you might as well wait for spring.

Because so many people park illegally on snow emergency streets, your chances of a tow are minimal during the day. There is more concern about keeping the streets as clear as possible for business and commuter traffic. The available tow trucks are busy with plowing and freeing stuck motorists and don't have time to deal with scofflaws like you. During the evening and night, however, there is less necessity to keep the streets clear, since there is less traffic, and towing begins en masse. In some of the wealthier suburbs which ban overnight parking to begin with, being towed is just about guaranteed. Make sure your car is off the street before settling down for the evening in front of the boob tube. With the streets clear of parked cars by about 4:00 A.M., the plows need go over the streets just one more time to have them ready for morning rush hour.

General Street Conditions

Like most things in life, the matter of plowing is mostly a matter of money. In the wealthy northern and western suburbs, equipment is ample, budgets adequate, parking bans enforced, and plowing finished just a few hours after the snow stops. Everywhere else in the metropolitan area, snow budgets would be adequate if only Boston were a tropical paradise. By mid-January (if not earlier), most communities are already dipping into next year's snow budget.

Plowing is fair to good on major streets of downtown Boston, Government Center, Kenmore Square, and most arteries going out to Allston, Brookline, Cambridge, and the major expressways. Parking bans are generally not enforced due to a shortage of tow trucks (see the discussion on snow emergencies above). The plowing job is often sloppy as a result, but the constant crunching of tires on the snow that remains eventually makes up for it.

On the residential streets of Boston and some surrounding communities the streets may not be plowed for two or three days, if at all. These streets are low priority, and there aren't enough plows to do the job any sooner. As for parking bans, forget about them. Nobody is going to wade through fourteen inches of snow to give you a ticket you won't pay, and the tow trucks will get stuck long before any of them can get their chains on your car.

By no means does the story end when the last plow has cleared the last street. In the suburbs, where an excellent plowing job is usually done, the streets are wide and parking is plentiful. A thin layer of packed snow generally persists, but the crews come back the first warm day with special machines to scrape it off. Such is life in suburbia.

In the major city streets, snow piles up around the parked cars that escaped towing during the snow emergency. This slows up traffic, but not too badly. The snow left by the plows is quickly chewed up by the constant roll of tires on it. The bright sunshine that usually follows a storm contributes as well, no matter how cold the temperature is.

In the case of the lonely residential streets, the storm continues to battle you long after it is over. Snow piles up on all sides of parked cars. If the street was never plowed, a thick "median" will develop on the street. You must drive your car in the snow tracks left by the other cars. If the street was plowed, the packed snow that remains has a habit of turning into ice. Traffic is usually reduced to one lane, and it is slow, slow, slow. If the street is two-way, it may be difficult to get by, as one car may have to pull into a driveway to give passage to an oncoming car. These streets get little traffic or sunlight, so the snow remains around much longer.

Proper parking space construction.

Parking Space Entry and Exit Techniques

In Chapter V we discussed techniques for finding parking. In the winter, there is the additional problem of threading your car into the space. This may sound trivial if you have never spent a winter in Boston, but rest assured it can be just as difficult to maneuver your car into two or three foot snowdrifts as it is to maneuver out of them.

Certain points of etiquette should be pointed out. The owner of a space during the storm retains "rights" to it for several days afterwards because he was the one who had to shovel out the space originally. The convention is that a garbage can claims a parking space during the winter. If you are foolish enough to remove someone's garbage can and take the space, you will be a sitting duck for slashed tires, stripping, or any of a thousand other fates you so richly deserve. Without this standard, the parking space could not be protected.

Parking is tight in winter, because so many spaces are lost to the snow. It is considered permissible to box in another car if you have to. If the car you box in cannot get out, that's his problem. If you are the one who's boxed in, however, it is perfectly OK to wipe out a good chunk of the bumper of the car that boxed you in. In the wintertime, all's fair in love and parking.

If the snow is deep, you may not be able to park parallel to the curb. This is no sweat unless you are blocking traffic. Remember that the traffic lane is much smaller, so you could have one end of your car four feet off the curb and still be OK. Don't block a driveway, though, unless it's only for a minute. If you do, your car is likely to end up on the dinner table of the local neighborhood towing company.

Track-in Approach

The easiest way to get into a parking space is to use the tracks made by the last car to leave. This usually means backing in. Ideally, your car will be about the same width as the tracks. If you're crazy and you have time,

energy, and a shovel, you might want to dig out the space, but this is seldom necessary unless the snow is at least a foot deep.

Blitz Approach

A deliberate and accurate approach to winter parking will get you nowhere. If the snow is more than three or four inches deep, you must gun the accelerator in order to build up some speed before crossing into the snow. Once you cross, you're almost sure to lose some control, skid, and probably get stuck. You must park in one move: if you stop, you will get stuck there. Don't touch the brake until you have either safely arrived in the parking space or wiped out the radiator of the car behind you. Don't worry about getting out of the space; save that for when you come back.

Getting Out

The most frustrating feeling that can be experienced by a Boston Driver is to have your car stuck in snow only inches away from the bare pavement on the main part of the road. Until you go those few inches, you can't go anywhere. Escaping is mostly a matter of gravity, friction, shoveling, and praying. But there are a few techniques that can help matters along.

The most reliable method of escaping from snow is to be pushed out. This is one time when there is no shame in getting by on a little help from your friends. Passing pedestrians will almost always give you a hand without even being asked. Never refuse anyone's offer: the more hands pushing the car, the merrier.

An easy escape from the magnetic snowdrifts is to park facing downhill. Gravity will do most of the work, with a *gentle* assist from the accelerator. The trouble with facing downhill is that if you get boxed in, you have almost no hope of getting out. If this happens, you should somehow push the other car far enough down the hill to give you the room you need. If all else fails, a series of love taps from your car to the other may

Burial victim.

If there are no other people around, you might try putting some rough material under the wheels to increase traction. Some things to try are an old towel, floor mats, the back seat upholstery, or a Bobby Orr T-shirt.

persuade it to get out of the way.

If your rear tires are in a rut of packed snow, you may have to use the rock-a-bye-baby approach. Put the car in gear and accelerate until the wheels spin. Now let up on the accelerator, and the car most likely will roll back into the rut. Repeat these two steps, going a little further each time, until you are out. Having someone to push your car greatly helps. You should be able to time perfectly the movement of the car and the accelerator pressure. Some clever drivers with automatic transmissions can keep shifting in synch from forward to reverse and back again, but this is usually just for show.

If you are stuck and can't free yourself, at least try to maneuver your car far enough into the street to block traffic. You will then find that plenty of other drivers are eager to help you. Don't worry: they're not motivated by any sort of good intentions; rather, they want to get you on the move so they can proceed themselves.

By far the most common and counterproductive method for extricating oneself is the "dentist's drill" approach. In this method the frustrated motorist guns the accelerator so hard that the wheels spin. The more they spin, the harder he guns the accelerator. The harder he guns the accelerator, the more the wheels spin. The dentist's drill can be heard on almost every street in Boston nearly every winter morning.

Don't you make the same mistake. Carried to extremes, the dentist's drill approach creates ice ruts so deep that you might just as well wait for baseball season to get your car out. If the dentist's drill doesn't get you out right away, you will have to stop, shovel some more around the wheels, and accelerate as slowly as possible out of the mess so as to create maximum traction. Just keep your cool, and save the dentist's drill for the dentist.

1. Accelerate.   2. Rock back.   3. Drive forward and out.

Winter Maneuvers

Since speed and maneuverability are considerably reduced during winter conditions, there are fewer opportunities to keep Boston Driving techniques sharp. But there are a few maneuvers that apply only to snow and ice which are worth discussing.

Turns

On an icy road surface, it is easy to go into a skid while making a turn. Since the road is so slippery, the steering wheel turns easily whether the car has power steering or not. The front wheels turn, but nobody tells the rear wheels to turn, so they keep going straight, and a skid results.

The standard driving school technique of turning into the direction of the skid might get you back in control of your car, but this method is clumsy and inele-

Turns on Ice

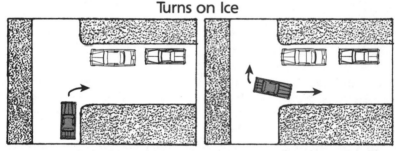

1. Accelerate into turn.

2. Lose control; rear wheels skid.

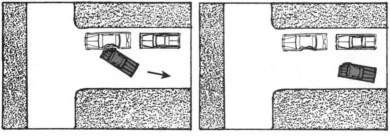

3. Bounce quietly off parked car; regain traction.

4. Finish.

gant because it often leaves you off to the side of the road out of the traffic stream. We favor a blitz approach: when your car begins to skid, hit the accelerator in an attempt to build up enough speed to drag the rear wheels through the turn. Usually the rear wheels will hit a patch of sand or bare pavement and push the car forward. Under ideal conditions, you might even burn some rubber. The worst thing that could possibly happen is that you might ram a parked car in a spot where it was already dented.

"Skitchers"

After a snow or ice storm, kids sometimes like to grab the rear bumper of a car when it stops at a light and be towed with their feet sliding along the ice. This is called skitching and is very dangerous for the kids. It is, however, no problem for you. Skitchers are simply aggressive pedestrians and should be treated as such. One thing you might try is coming to a *slow* stop, then getting out of your car and chasing them away. This is unlikely to convince them who's boss, so more drastic measures are generally called for. We favor a sudden acceleration while pretending not to notice that they're there. This is fighting fire with fire and will usually convince the skitcher to let go. If all else fails, you can go into reverse to get rid of a skitcher or two, but make sure your license plates are obscured by snow, just in case anyone is watching.

One-Way Streets

If you are thinking about going the wrong way on a one-way street during a big blizzard, by all means go right ahead. Since you will be the only one foolish enough to be out on the street in such bad weather, you should have no problems.

Stop Signs and Intersections

On an icy road forget about stop signs, since you can't stop anyway. If the road is covered with thick snow, it is a mistake to stop just because you see a stop sign. If you do so, you may find yourself stuck, or at best it might take a while to accelerate back up to speed. This also applies to red lights, especially at night when all sane persons are already home.

CHAPTER SEVEN

Advanced maneuvers

By reading the first six chapters of this book, you have acquired all the basic skills necessary to become a first-rate Boston Driver. You could stop right here and drive happily ever after, but you would miss out on some of the fine points that separate the mere expert drivers from the superstars. This chapter describes some advanced maneuvers and harassment techniques that you can use as desired to obtain an edge over your fellow Boston Drivers. Most of the maneuvers described in this chapter are expansions on the basic maneuvers covered in chapter III, which should now be a routine part of your Boston Driving repertoire.

You might wonder why you need to learn to harass your fellow Boston Drivers. "After all," you might say, "they don't harass me." Unfortunately, this simply is not true. Every time you are the victim of a commonplace cutoff, sidesqueeze, or block, you have been harassed. Whenever someone beats you to a lonely parking space or double-parks in your lane of traffic, you have likewise become the object of harassment, intentional or not. There is often very little you can do about this type of treatment. However, the best defense is a good offense: do unto others before they do unto you. Remember, it's nothing personal. You're just playing the Boston Driving game the way it was meant to be played.

Many of the maneuvers described in this chapter are not widely known at present; therefore, we suggest that you use a certain amount of discretion when executing them. Overuse of these techniques could tip off other drivers who have not yet acquired these valuable skills. Even tourists catch on sooner or later. When these techniques become too widely known, there is a lesser chance of success when applying them.

Taxicabs

When it comes to Boston Driving, nobody does it better than your typical neighborhood cab driver. He can cut off in his sleep and blast through yellow and red lights with surgical precision. Cabbies' driving ability should always be respected, but they can act extremely belligerent toward other drivers at times. Counter-harassment measures are often called for, but watch it: most cab drivers carry a set of tire irons with them, and they're not always used for changing tires.

While the cab drivers themselves are very tough individuals, their vehicles certainly are not. Since cab companies collect no fares on an idle car, they naturally try to keep their fleets in service as close to twenty-four hours per day as possible. This means that when a cab comes in limping after a twelve-hour shift, there is only time enough for a quick first-aid job. In some of the larger garages, this treatment is usually applied by the company mechanic, who is well-trained in the art of bubble-gum-and-spit repair. After thirty years or 300,000 miles (whichever comes first), the cab is probably even less roadworthy than it looks. Most cabbies know that in the event of a collision their cars will more than likely turn to dust. Seasoned Boston Drivers realize this and make the most of it.

In good traffic and in bad, taxi drivers love to tailgate. The alert Boston Driver can turn this weakness into an advantage and get a few laughs out of it besides. The cabbie tailgates because he is extremely impatient. If he finds himself behind you in traffic, he will try to intimidate you into yielding. Don't even consider letting him by; slow down and hold your lane. When he becomes irritated enough to try to pass you, he will change lanes, and you do the same. If you time it properly, he will still be behind you going 10 or 15 m.p.h. slower than he wants. When he tries to switch back, you switch back as well. After playing this game for a while, he will get the message that you are deliberately harassing him. If you look in your rearview mirror at this point, you may be able to see the steam rising from his collar. When he is finally able to accelerate by you, give him a big grin as he passes, and his blood pressure will climb right through the roof. You can then bask in the satisfaction of having taken years off the cabbie's life.

Cab drivers do not always try to leave you behind in a cloud of dust, however. Cabbies have been known to go unbearably slowly when they are "cruising" for fares. Worse, if they spot a live customer, they will go to any lengths to pick him up. This could include an abrupt stop, sudden lane changes, or even a U-turn into a convenient double-parking space. If one of these creatures crosses your path, give him a couple of long blasts on your horn. It may not get him to move, but it will certainly make you feel better, and it may make him squirm a little bit.

In some of the heavier trafficked parts of town, taxi stands offer convenient illegal parking. By now you realize that a parking ticket is not what you should be worried about. To a cab driver, a taxi stand is holy ground. If you park in one for any length of time, you are likely to find out what those tire irons are really used for.

Tread not in the pathway of a taxicab, lest its driver wreak vengeance upon thee with his tire iron.

Cadillacs

Wealthy, obnoxious, and invariably inept, Cadillac owners view the world through the portals of their very own Sherman Tanks. By "Cadillac" we are referring to not only the traditional oversize models, but also the Lincoln Continental and any other cars in the general pimpmobile class.

In the Boston area, where small cars were in vogue long before the 1973 Arab oil embargo, Caddies make an even more obvious spectacle of themselves than they do elsewhere. Since they are the biggest and grossest cars on the road, their overpampered owners feel they are entitled to special road hogging privileges. They look upon non-Caddy owners as second class citizens who must yield on demand and who are unfit even to polish their bumpers. They are also atrocious Boston Drivers since they rely on their bulk for everything. They would fare much better if they took advantage of the extra power, stability, and durability they paid for, but they never do.

Even if you have no idea what a Cadillac looks like, you can easily spot one on the highway. Caddies love to get in the left lane and go 20 m.p.h. below the speed limit. If you should hap-

pen to pass one on the right, however, don't be surprised if the Cadillac driver suddenly and briefly snaps back to reality, accelerates to 80 m.p.h., and passes you back with a contemptuous sneer and a cloud of premium exhaust. Apparently, they consider it a personal affront to be passed by any car worth less than $15,000. They then slow back down to 40 m.p.h., as if the whole incident never happened. To understand the reason for this strange, but typical Cadillac behavior, you will simply have to go out and buy one yourself.

Occasionally you will see a Cadillac barreling down the highway at a constant speed of 75 m.p.h. or more. This indicates that the cruise control is engaged, and the driver is therefore busy mixing drinks while watching the news on his onboard Sony Trinitron. If you should happen to be in the same lane going slower than he, it is inevitable that you will be plowed under by two tons of the finest and shiniest Detroit has to offer. Even if you should get his attention through use of your horn or some wild gesture, it will do you no good. No Cadillac driver worth his salt would ever consider braking because doing so would disengage the cruise control and force him to drive. If you should see the Tank in your rear view mirror gaining on you, waste no time changing lanes, and you may live to make your next car insurance payment.

Cadillacs are easy to spot in the city as well. Although they are not generally too wide for a single lane, their drivers obviously think they are. On major city streets having four lanes, a Cadillac driver will require at least two of them. The reason for this is that he needs sufficient buffer between himself, the parked cars on the right, and the oncoming traffic to his left. If he wants to change lanes or make a turn and you are in his way, he will move slowly toward you as if you are not there. When he does turn, he always cuts his left turns and takes his right turns so wide he has to start from the left lane. Even the worst MBTA bus drivers can execute neater turns than a Cadillac driver. And finally, when he is lucky enough to find a street parking space big enough to suit his needs, the Cadillac driver demonstrates that he has no conception whatsoever of parallel parking. Most of the time he simply drives forward into the space, leaving the rear end of the car sticking out into traffic.

Despite the physical advantages of Cadillacs and the obnoxious behavior of their drivers, the skilled Boston Driver will have little difficulty handling these dinosaurs of the road. While Cadillac drivers do like to execute intimidating maneuvers, they do it out of insecurity, just like a typical street bully. The simple truth is that at the slightest threat of a cutoff or sidesqueeze, they will yield. Their fatal weakness is that they are deathly afraid of an accident. After all, it might scratch the paint, and that would be a severe blow to the Caddy owner's ego. In the event

large dose of your horn. Sitting in his mink-lined, gas-guzzling, environmentally-controlled fortress, the driver is not likely to hear it.

of a showdown between a late model Cadillac and your 1965 Ford Falcon, it is clear who has more to lose. After all, your Falcon is not going to need $5,000 worth of body work after a collison; chances are, it won't look too different from before.

Because of their bulk and the cowardly nature of their drivers, you will find Cadillacs to be the easiest cars on the road to block. The only thing guaranteed not to work against a Cadillac is a

Volkswagen Beetles

Volkswagen stopped producing the Beetle in 1976, but there are still plenty of them polluting the roads. Beetles are as obnoxious as Cadillacs, but in a different way. No self-respecting Boston Driver would willingly pass up an opportunity to swat one of these Bugs.

Beetle owners think that the compactness and good maneuverability of their cars give them special license to manipulate traffic for their purposes. While the Cadillac owner's philosophy is "I can do what I want because I'm bigger than you," the VW Beetle owner sees it as "I can do what I want because you can't catch me." The power resulting from a high first-gear ratio gives them an ability to pull away from a stop as well as most high-powered sports cars. Favorite Bug maneuvers are quick cutoffs and lane changes both on the highway and on city streets. Their small wheelbase gives them exceptional ability to weave. They can make turns very rapidly around a small radius as well; this makes it fairly easy for them to execute beat-the-green left turns (see Chapter III, "Basic Left Turns"). "Bug" is certainly an apt nickname for these cars: they're constantly darting and poking and swirling like the gnats in your face on a warm summer evening.

Because of the inherent quickness and maneuverability of the Beetle, the Boston Driver must keep his basic skills sharper than ever when confronting one of these insects on wheels. The Beetle's weakness is that, like the Cadillac, it cannot afford an accident. While the Caddy owner worries about chipping the paint, the Beetle owner worries about himself and his car turning into a blob of chopped meat and tin foil. With the engine mounted in the rear of these featherweight cars, all that protects the driver in the event of a front end collision is some sheet metal, air, and prayer. Therefore, the best defense against a Bug is to make the driver think that its wings are about to be clipped. If one is weaving around you, close the "guillotine" (see Chapter III, "Weaving"). Even if you are unable to actually prevent him from getting through, you can still enjoy the satisfaction of making him sweat. If a Beetle in an oncoming lane tries to sneak a left turn across your lane in front of you, show your savvy by rushing the intersection and making it close. As the Bug driver goes by, assault him with the longest and loudest blast your horn can muster. This may scare him enough to make him think twice before attempting such a stunt again—especially in Boston.

Since Volkswagen is no longer selling Beetles in this country, their numbers on U.S. highways

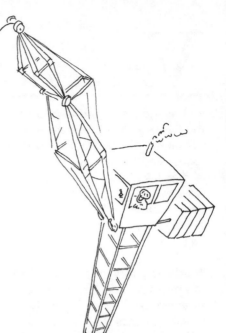

have been slowly dropping; consequently, there have been fewer and fewer Bugs around to bug. As is usually the case when a technological vacuum has developed, the Japanese were ready and willing to fill the void. Almost as soon as the manufacture of new Bugs stopped, Honda Civics began to roll off the assembly lines in ever increasing numbers. These cars are similar to the Bug in size and weight, and their drivers exhibit similar behavior. In every important aspect, Honda Civics have become the Japanese Beetles of the 1980s, thus assuring a generous supply of cars to harass for many years to come.

Advanced Turns

In Chapter III we discussed basic left turns and U-turns. These techniques should suffice for most common situations. After mastering the additional refinements described in this section, you will have the capability to turn anywhere, anytime, under any conditions.

Turn from the Wrong Lane

Even the most well-prepared Boston Driver will occasionally face the problem of making a left turn from the right lane or a right turn from the left lane (or any turn from the center lane of a three-lane road). This can happen even when he knows his route thoroughly and has made the same trip many times before. Most of the time, however, the situation arises because the driver is uncertain about which way to turn, or he arrives at his desired intersection before he expects to. Without a working knowledge of techniques for wrong-lane turns, the helpless driver will needlessly waste precious time circling around in an attempt to correct his mistake.

We must point out that the attempt is often futile since the street layout of the Boston area is such that retracing one's tracks takes at least forty-five minutes, if it is possible at all.

When you are confronted with the necessity of making a turn from the wrong lane, the simplest solution is to "slip in." This is accomplished by executing a routine cutoff or sidesqueeze to get into the proper lane, time permitting. If absolutely necessary, you could slow down to buy additional time. The slip-in maneuver should be applied when you are sure you are in the wrong lane and want to take corrective action.

On the other hand, if you are on a road with two lanes in each direction and you are approaching your turn unsure of whether you want to go left or right, the best course of action is to execute a block by straddling the two lanes (see Chapter III, "Blocking"). This should prevent any cars from trying to pass you, giving you the option of waiting until the last possible moment to make up your mind which way to turn.

If the road is three lanes in each direction, however, the situation is more complicated because traditional blocking alone will not do the job. We recommend the Guerrilla Blocking Tactic introduced to Boston by a noted Southeast Asian cab driver now living in Southie. When executing the Guerrilla Blocking Tactic, it is absolutely essential to weave so wildly that other drivers become convinced you are drunk. The effect is enhanced if the other drivers can see you clutching a can of beer as you lie slumped over the steering wheel. As you get closer to the intersection, block the two right lanes while signalling a left turn (or vice-versa). If any drivers still had any notions of trying to squeeze by you up to this point, this open-field tactic should put an end to them.

Even if you run completely out of time and find yourself at the intersection still in the wrong lane, don't give up. If your light is green—or if there is no light—simply pull into the intersection, stop, and wait for your break. It is true that the cars behind you will have to either wait for you or go around you, but that's their problem. Under no circumstances should you allow horn honking or verbal abuse from other drivers to intimidate you into aborting your successful strategy.

If the light is red, and cars are stopped at the intersection, the problem becomes one of jockey-

Guerrilla Blocking Tactic

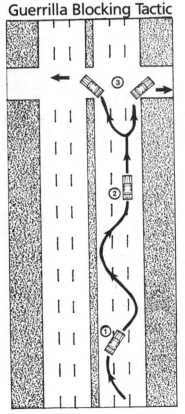

1. Weave wildly to scare off other drivers.
2. Block two lanes near intersection.
3. Make your move left or right.

Standing Cutoff

  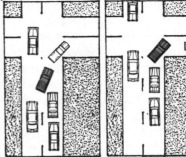

| 1. Start. | 2. Establish position in other lane; wait for green light. | 3. When space permits, pull completely into other lane. | 4. Finish turn from proper lane. |

ing for position. You will usually have plenty of time to decide on a strategy while waiting for the light to change. At worst you can stay where you are, wait for the green light, and proceed into the intersection as described above. A superior method that will almost always work is the "standing cutoff." This maneuver is executed by inching the front of your car ahead of another vehicle stopped in the adjacent lane. Once you have established position you have done the hard part. The cars behind you in both directions are now blocked. When the light changes to green and traffic ahead of you begins to move, simply complete the cutoff of the car you have already nosed out; you will seldom encounter any real resistance. Be profes-

sional and businesslike about it. There is no need to look back and gloat over the frustration written all over the faces of your victims.

Oncoming Traffic Left Turns

In most cities, executing a left turn can be one of the most time-consuming and frustrating of all driving exercises. However, in Boston, decades of research have produced several innovative procedures for dealing with this problem. One of the best is referred to as the Oncoming Traffic Left Turn.

The essence of the Oncoming Traffic Left Turn is not that it is made from the *wrong* lane, but that it is made from the *oncom-*

ing lane—on the other side of the double line. This technique is applicable when you are in line for a left turn, but stymied because the lead driver doesn't have what it takes to cut across the traffic and finish off his left turn. No doubt he is an out-of-state Cadillac driver who is visiting Boston for the first time. When confronting this situation, you must pull into the oncoming lane, rush the intersection, and cut him off to complete your left turn. Naturally, this maneuver is risky since any oncoming traffic that slips through the intersection could place you in an embarassing position with no possible escape. Therefore, the maneuver should be executed as quickly as possible. The best time to move is when the lead car finally begins his own left turn, thereby blocking the oncoming lanes.

Properly applied, the Oncoming Lane Left Turn can save the alert Boston Driver a great deal of time. In addition to the situation described above, this maneuver may be used any time the first car in line fails to move, whatever the reason. For example, the lead car could be stalled or broken down. More likely, the confused turkey driving the lead car will suddenly decide he doesn't really want to turn left after all, and he finds he can't go straight either because he is in a left-turn-only lane or because the intersection is already

Oncoming Lane Left Turn

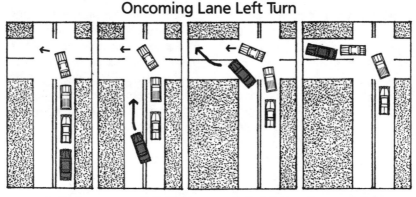

1. Start.   2. Pull into oncoming lane.   3. Rush intersection; cut off lead car.   4. Finish.

clogged with traffic. So he sits there, and so do you—until you make your move into the oncoming lane. One final situation where you should consider using this maneuver is whenever you see two fourteen-year-old boys get out and run away from a shiny new sports car. If they leave the doors open and the motor running, and you can hear police sirens in the distance, it's a good bet the car is going nowhere fast.

Gas Station Turns

In Chapter III we discussed how valuable gas stations can be in assisting the Boston Driver in making U-turns. This is only one of dozens of possible uses of gas stations in advanced Boston Driving. (Where no gas station is available, vacant lots and small shopping centers can sometimes be used instead.) This section will demonstrate that there are certainly many other uses for gas stations besides filling up your tank.

Right Turns

This is the simplest of the gas station maneuvers; it is recommended for Boston Drivers who are trying these techniques for the first time. It is most commonly used to avoid waiting in a long line of traffic to take a right turn. When proceeding slower than you'd like toward the inter-

section, simply pull into a convenient corner gas station. Pass by the pumps and pretend to look disgusted at the prices; this gives you the excuse you need to continue to the opposite driveway, from which you can turn onto the cross street. If the station is doing a good business that day, you might have to execute some simple cutoffs and blocking maneuvers to get through. Of course, you didn't really need gas right then anyway; the whole purpose of this act is to legitimize your detour through the station. You will probably save yourself many minutes this way. While there is some question as to whether this maneuver is legal or not, it has become a standard Boston Driving procedure. It is also the basic element of the more complex gas station maneuvers to be described in subsequent para-

Gas Station Right Turn

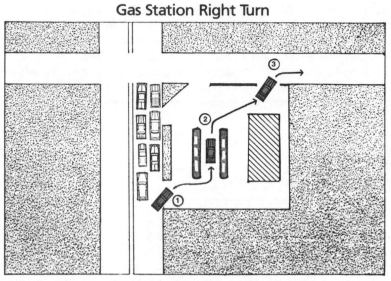

1. Turn into gas station.
2. Pause at pumps.
3. Continue to opposite exit and turn.

graphs.

Oncoming Traffic/Gas Station Left Turn Combination

When executing an oncoming lane left turn, always give a quick glance to the left to see whether there is a gas station on the near corner. If so, you can complete your turn faster and easier with less risk. You begin this maneuver in the usual way by pulling into the oncoming traffic lane. Proceed into the gas station up to the pumps. As before, "change your mind" about getting gas and drive to the opposite entrance to the station. Make a simple left turn or a Boston Left Turn onto the cross street, and you can chalk up another several minutes saved through expert technique. Leave all the worries of red and green lights and nasty opposing traffic to all those cars that were formerly ahead of you and are still waiting to get through.

Straight-Ahead-on-Red

The introduction of right-turn-on-red has opened the doors for many innovations in urban driving techniques. In Massachusetts this has been carried a step further: expert Boston Drivers are now successfully engineering straight-ahead-on-red maneuvers (without incurring any unwanted moving violations, of course). The straight-ahead-on-red maneuver is a combination of a simple gas station right turn and basic left and right turn. Essentially, all that is involved is to turn into the gas station (and decide you don't need gas), proceed to the opposite driveway, make a left onto the cross street (which has a green light) and a right onto your original street. This is ideal for intersections with long light cycles, at times when you see the light change to red as you arrive. If the light should change back to green before you complete the right turn onto your original street, you will be facing a red light on the cross street. This may present a problem if heavy traffic from your original direction makes it more difficult for you to pull off a right-turn-on-red. However, this is an excellent opportunity to brush up on your cutoff and sidesqueeze technique. You may also be lucky enough to find another friendly gas station through which to turn right.

If the left turn out of the gas station is blocked by a median or by dense traffic, you will instead have to make a right turn out of the station, followed by a U-turn, to achieve the same effect. This, of course, takes more time and therefore presents a greater risk of missing the light. However, there are dozens of intersections throughout the greater Boston area whose light cycles are so long that any drunk driver could effortlessly execute these turns five times within a single cycle, and many do so just for fun.

Straight-Ahead-on-Red Maneuver

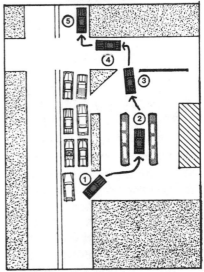

1. Turn into gas station.
2. Pause at pumps.
3. Proceed to opposite exit.
4. Turn left onto cross street.
5. Turn right onto original street.

Left-Turn-on-Red

A variation on the straight-ahead-on-red maneuver described above can be used to execute left turns on red as well. The only caveat is that the turn must be started from the right lane (i.e., the wrong lane). It is performed by executing a straight-ahead-on-red maneuver, but omitting the final right turn so as to proceed directly through the intersection on the cross street.

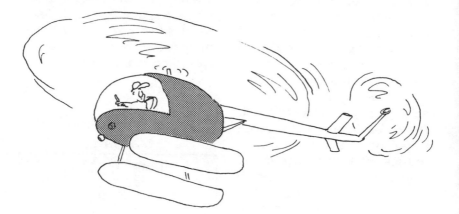

Sidewalk Driving and Sidewalk Parking

Many drivers, even some good-to-excellent Boston Drivers, suffer from the misconception that sidewalks are off-limits to them. However, sidewalks are no less a part of the skilled Boston Driver's equipment than his steering wheel. After all, pedestrians walk on your streets, why shouldn't you drive on their sidewalks?

There are a surprising number of situations where it can be quite advantageous to go up on the sidewalk. For example, a sidewalk can be used in place of a gas station or empty lot to pass a slow car ahead of you. Simply roll up over the curb, accelerate forward while on the sidewalk (carefully avoiding trees, parking meters, pedestrians, and other hazards), and squeeze back into the traffic stream when convenient. Sidewalks are ideal for avoiding large, deep potholes, especially the kind that would engulf your entire front end. Sidewalks can also be used to skirt around construction sites, loading and unloading trucks, and block parties. A final situation where you might need a sidewalk is when you are going down a one-way street the wrong way. If another car should have the audacity to come down the street the right way, you might have to pull onto the sidewalk to let him by. An incidental benefit of this approach is that once you are on the sidewalk, you are no longer going the wrong way, since sidewalk traffic is always permitted in both directions.

On crowded city streets, every last bit of space must be considered for its parking potential, and this certainly includes sidewalks. Consider the advantages: they bring you directly to your doorstep, and there is never a meter. They are a convenient last resort when no other parking is available. On narrow, one-lane roads (e.g., Beacon Hill) where there is not enough room to park in the street without obstructing traffic, sidewalk parking is the answer. In doing so, you run much less risk of falling into the jaws of the not-so-friendly neighborhood tow truck. As long as you are not obstructing traffic, you are not likely to be bothered. Furthermore, you don't have to worry about moving your car on street cleaning days since you aren't on the street anymore. Other than the street cleaning situation, it is seldom necessary to get all four wheels up on the sidewalk; straddling the curb with two wheels up and two down is usually sufficient. In the winter, when the snow prevents you from seeing where the street ends and the sidewalk begins, you may consider them to be one and the same for parking purposes. This is necessary because the snow takes up so much of the available parking (and driving) area; therefore, you can park anywhere with impunity.

One final note on sidewalk driving: for those who are collecting points, keep in mind that hitting anyone on the sidewalk is worth an additional two bonus points over and above the standard point values given in Chapter IV.

Deceptive Use of Signals

Every car comes equipped with a number of built-in signalling devices, including directional signals, a horn, high-beam headlights, and flashers. However, few drivers know how to make optimum use of this equipment in achieving their Boston Driving goals. These tools are at your fingertips whenever you are behind the wheel; don't overlook their potential for expediting your trip, as well as for harassing your fellow Boston Drivers.

Directionals

Besides their normal use of notifying other drivers of your intention to make a left or right turn, directionals have several other uses as well. Actually, most drivers misuse their directionals by signalling way too early. It is best not to signal until the middle of the turn; that way, your legal obligation to signal has been fulfilled, but no one has time to react.

Your directionals can also be used in the situation where you want to harass and ultimately shake off a tailgater. When being followed too closely for comfort, signal a lane change and then gradually decelerate without actually changing lanes. At first, the tailgater will be reluctant to pass you, since he will think you are about to switch lanes yourself, and he will have to slow down. By the time you are down to about 10 m.p.h., he will get the message, pass you, and be out of your life forever. Or, you can speed up and tailgate him if it suits your fancy (see Chapter III, "Tailgating").

Another possible opportunity occurs when you are in an unfamiliar part of town looking for a particular street to turn into. As you approach each intersection, you signal a turn (it doesn't really matter whether you signal left or right). If the intersection contains the street you are looking for, you turn and end the matter. Otherwise, you continue on straight, leaving your confused fellow drivers to guess at your real intentions. Since they don't know when you are going to turn, or which way, or even whether you're going to turn at

all, they are likely to give you run of the road. This is ideal when you don't know yourself which way you will want to turn when you reach your desired street. It is especially effective when combined with the Guerrilla Blocking Tactic described earlier in this chapter.

A final use of the directional is to announce that you have completed a cutoff. Just as you are pulling in front of your victim, signal briefly just to let him know you're there. Of course, he knew that already, so your signal is just a way of rubbing it in. This is the Boston Driving equivalent of the Red Auerbach victory cigar.

Horn

Horns were originally intended to give the driver a means to warn other drivers or pedestrians of a potentially hazardous situation. However, in routine Boston

Driving, horns are never used for this purpose. As the reader is surely aware by now, warning other drivers of one's intentions is the road to Boston Driving ruin. In the current environment, horns are used strictly for recreation, intimidation, and harassment.

The most basic use of a horn is to persuade drivers in front of you at an intersection to get moving after a light turns green. One second is the maximum amount of reaction time you should tolerate before blasting away. While the leading drivers may not be able to go right away due to cross traffic running the red light, this is their problem, not yours. After all, you have better things to do with your time than to spend all day stuck at a green light. If you have ever been the lead car under such circumstances, you know how intense the pressure of hundreds of horns honking behind you can be, especially when there is no clear path in front of you. For the unfortunate sap who stalls his car in this situation, it's all over.

Another common use of the horn is to deter another driver from executing a cutoff against you. The experienced Boston Driver should be aware of and on the lookout for the telltale signs of a cutoff, so that he can honk some sense into the opposing driver. These include edging slowly toward your lane, passing you, looking directly at you or your car, and (strictly for novices) signalling. Your blast of horn must authoritatively convey the message that (1) you are not going to let him in front of you, and (2) he should revise his driving plans accordingly. You must time your blast properly, for if you are late, he will have already cut you off. In this case your horn wil do no more than call attention to other drivers that you have been whipped.

You should take advantage of every opportunity to honk your horn to intimidate pedestrians as well. They don't even have to be in the street: if one threatens to step off the curb toward your path, you should immediately speed up and give a long, loud blast. If you execute quickly and

effectively, your pedestrian victim will most likely beat a hasty retreat back onto the sidewalk. Acting drunk or out of control will increase your chances of success. If, in spite of your best efforts, a pedestrian does get into the street, the same strategy can be applied. In this case, your long, loud blast of horn is intended to encourage him to hurry up so that you won't have to brake for him as you speed by.

Finally, Boston Drivers have traditionally used their horns to commemorate happy occasions. For example, horn concerts can be heard in Kenmore Square after every Red Sox win. They are also used to celebrate New Year's Eve, Friday afternoon at 5:00, and any other event worth noting. For some reason, these horn-honking celebrations always seem to occur at times when traffic is jammed, and no one has anything better to do. Rumor has it that this practice

will cease when the Red Sox win their next World Series; it has been going on since they won their last one in 1918.

Flashers

If you followed the car-shopping advice in Chapter I, you might have actually found a car that does not have flashers. (By "flashers" we are referring to taillights blinking in unison, not dirty old men in trenchcoats.) However, they have been standard equipment for about fifteen years now, so the vast majority of cars will be equipped with them. In effect, flashers are a visual horn; they are intended to signal that the driver is doing something unusual or is in trouble. In the world of Boston Driving, however, everyone else is in trouble if your flashers are on. They convey the intimidating message that you are executing an offensive driving maneuver, and other drivers had best stay clear.

Flashers might be used if you are going much faster or slower than other traffic. When you are on the highway going 20 m.p.h. faster than the traffic stream, flashers make weaving considerably easier. When driving slowly, you can use flashers to facilitate cruising for parking or to enhance the Guerrilla Blocking Tactic (see discussion under "Turn from Wrong Lane"). In the latter case, flashers signal a left and a right turn simultaneously, so you're covered, regardless of which way you decide to turn.

Another good time to use flashers is when you feel the urge to drive onto the sidewalk (see the discussion on "Sidewalk Driving" earlier in this chapter). In this case, the flashers provide adequate notice to pedestrians to get out of your way.

One final use of flashers is in manufacturing a parking space where absolutely no other is available. The combination of a raised hood and flashers guarantees thirty minutes of free parking anywhere in the city, including the Governor's space under the statehouse.

High Beams

High-beam headlights can be used not only for lighting up the roadway on a dark night but also as an offensive driving tool. Most drivers will do almost anything to avoid the stinging, blinding glare of these lights, even if it requires them to slow down or yield. It is a common practice to blink your high beams at an oncoming driver who may inadvertently have his own high beams on and aimed at you. If he does not immediately switch to low beams, you can leave your high beams on so as to do unto him as he has done unto you. Most drivers get the message sooner or later, however.

High beams can also work wonders in clearing the left lane of slow-moving traffic, especially Cadillacs. Tailgate as closely as possible before lighting up the entire car with your high beams. Your victims will hopefully get the impression that you are giving them the third degree. Because of the blinding glare, they can't see you, but you can see them perfectly well. Few drivers can withstand more than a few seconds of such intimidation before yielding. If you flash your lights on and off, they might even think you're the police and pull over, expecting the worst. Once your lane is clear, leave your high beams on to light up the roadway in front of you. In effect, you have "claimed" that road space for your own personal use. Anyone who would then wander into it would do so at his own risk.

For those who are collecting points, high beams can make your target victims stand out on a dark night. Many pedestrians freeze momentarily when they see bright lights shined directly at them; this makes the pickings even easier.

All of the Above

The simultaneous use of high beams, horn, and flashers looks and sounds like an emergency. Nothing instills fear into the hearts of drivers quite like the sight of a car barreling toward them with high beams and flashers on, horn blaring, and a madman behind the wheel. They will usually get out of your way as fast as they can. This technique is especially useful for traveling at top speed down the "middle lane" of the Callahan Tunnel when you have only ten minutes to catch a 5:30 P.M. flight out of Logan Airport. You might also try this if you are mired in Kenmore Square after an extra-inning ballgame and late for an important dinner appointment. It stands to reason that this maneuver should be applied sparingly, lest its impact be diluted from overuse. Short of installing a police siren and a bubble gum machine on top of your car, this is the most potent medicine available to Boston Drivers. It will enable you to cut through the worst traffic jams like a hot knife through butter.

Hand Signals

During driver training, you were probably taught to use hand signals as an alternative to directionals to tell other drivers where you are going. However, in the Boston area, hand signals are used to tell other drivers where to go. Unlike on the football field, Boston Drivers are never called for "illegal use of the hands." Hand signals may not get you ahead of opposing drivers, but they are a widely-used harassment technique. While the extended middle finger remains the most popular hand signal, there are literally hundreds of other forms, with new ones being invented every day. This is one reason why most Boston Drivers prefer the summer months: with the windows routinely open, they can extend their hands on a moment's notice. The practice of giving hand signals is so popular that many stores now sell phosphorescent gloves for night signalling. Further research on the subject will undoubtedly produce many techniques for communicating with hand signals in the years to come.

The Twenty Best Accident Excuses of All Time

If you have ever been in an accident you may have had trouble describing it on your insurance claim form. Below are actual accident descriptions from twenty people who had no trouble whatsoever.

1. To avoid hitting the bumper of the car in front, I struck the pedestrian.

2. An invisible car came out of nowhere, struck my car, and vanished.

3. I was on my way to the doctor with rear end trouble when my universal joint gave way, causing me to have an accident.

4. The guy was all over the road. I had to swerve a number of times before I hit him.

5. In my attempt to kill a fly, I drove into a telephone pole.

6. I had been shopping for plants all day and was on my way home. As I reached an intersection, a hedge sprang up obscuring my vision and I did not see the other car.

7. I collided with a stationary truck coming the other way.

8. I had been driving for forty years when I fell asleep at the wheel and had an accident.

9. As I approached the intersection, a sign suddenly appeared in a place where no stop sign had ever appeared before. I was unable to stop in time to avoid the accident.

10. I was thrown from my car as it left the road. I was later found in a ditch by some cows.

11. Coming home I drove into the wrong house and collided with a tree I didn't have.

12. The telephone pole was approaching. I was attempting to swerve out of its way when it struck the front end.

13. The other car collided with mine without giving warning of its intentions.

14. The truck backed through my windshield into my wife's face.

15. I thought my window was down, but I found out it was up when I put my head through it.

16. The pedestrian hit me and went under my car.

17. The pedestrian had no idea which direction to run, so I ran over him.

18. I pulled away from the side of the road, glanced at my mother-in law, and headed over the embankment.

19. I was sure the old fellow would never make it to the other side of the road when I struck him.

20. I saw a slow-moving, sad-faced old gentleman as he bounced off the roof of my car.

Final Exam

Test your Boston Driving knowledge by taking this ten-question, multiple-choice examination. It might highlight some weak spots in your training that you should brush up on. Answers and scoring instructions may be found following the test.

1. You are trying to pull out of a parking space, but your car does not move. You hear a whirring sound outside your car window. This indicates:

   (A) your dentist has opened an outdoor office.
   (B) boating season is here.
   (C) it's wintertime in Boston.
   (D) it's garbage pickup day.

2. Filene's is having a once-in-a-lifetime sale on lingerie on the Saturday before Christmas. You arrive on the scene five minutes before closing and can't find a legitimate parking space. What should you do?

   (A) Double park, raise your hood, put your flashers on, and run inside.
   (B) Try to bribe the nearest girl scout on the sidewalk to pick up some choice items for you.
   (C) Give up and go home.
   (D) Drive through the main entrance, take a right at the second cash register, and follow to the lingerie dept.

3. Boston streets were the result of:

   (A) the volcanic eruption of Mt. Bunker in 250 B.C.
   (B) seventeenth-century cowpaths.
   (C) an early resident's love of spaghetti.
   (D) a conscientious and comprehensive urban plan.

4. Which of the following is the best car for Boston Driving?

   (A) a brand new Audi 5000, with the sticker still on it
   (B) a 1965 Ford Falcon with 180,000 miles on it, no hubcaps, a burned out muffler, and liberal rust
   (C) a 1980 Pontiac Trans-Am
   (D) a late model Sherman Tank, fully equipped with howitzers and machine guns

5. A sidesqueeze is:

   (A) a method for merging into dense streams of traffic.
   (B) a sandwich served at Elsie's.
   (C) a way to go between two parked cars.
   (D) a nice thing to happen on a date.

6. The Boston Police pull you over for driving the wrong way down Berkeley Street at rush hour. What is the most likely outcome?

   (A) They will charge you with drunk driving, arrest you, and impound your car.
   (B) They will issue you a ticket for driving the wrong way down a one-way street.
   (C) They will give you a warning for having a broken taillight.
   (D) They will ask you what you think of the Celtics' chances this year.

7. Back Street is a good place to go to:

   (A) park in a tow zone.
   (B) travel rapidly through Back Bay.
   (C) avoid snowdrifts.
   (D) get mugged.

8. You receive a $25 ticket for parking in a tow zone. You should:

   (A) pay it and be thankful you weren't towed.
   (B) pay $10 and hope they take it.
   (C) take the case to the Supreme Court.
   (D) leave it on your windshield and park in the same place the next day.

9. The chains carried in the trunk of most taxicabs are:

(A) deadly weapons to ensure traffic justice.
(B) only used during the winter.
(C) good for towing other cars or stubborn passengers.
(D) a gift for the cabbie's girlfriend.

10. The "Beat-the-Green" technique is:

(A) a recipe for making pureed vegetables.
(B) a way to go straight ahead on red.
(C) a quick left turning technique.
(D) rarely successful against the Celtics.

ANSWERS

1. C	6. C
2. A	7. D
3. B	8. D
4. B	9. A
5. A	10. C

SCORING

9 – 10 correct:	Allston Cab Driver
7 – 8 correct:	City Commuter
4 – 6 correct:	Suburban Weekender
0 – 3 correct:	Hopeless Tourist

About the Authors

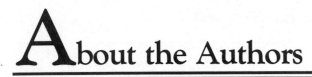

Ira Gershkoff showed his aptitude for Boston Driving at a very early age, when he developed the habit of crossing the street, then looking both ways. A native of Haverhill, Massachusetts, Mr. Gershkoff's Boston Driving career began in 1968, when he drove himself and a friend to a Bruins' game at Boston Garden, got lost on the way home, and ran out of gas. From that auspicious beginning, his career blossomed to the point that in 1976 he set a single season record by collecting 1,272 unpaid parking tickets without a single moving violation. Mr. Gershkoff now works as a consultant to the Federal Aviation Administration, where he is currently doing research on the application of Boston Driving techniques to air traffic control.

While growing up in New York City, **Richard Trachtman** gave himself an early taste of Boston driving experience by engineering catastrophic collisions on his H-O scale road racing set. However, Mr. Trachtman began Boston Driving in earnest in the fall of 1970, when he enrolled at M.I.T. and moved to the Boston area. Within a few months he had abandoned a promising career in astrophysics to sign on as a night driver for Boston Cab Co. In the years that followed, he logged nearly half a million miles carrying everything from drunken sailors bound for the Combat Zone to urine samples bound for the laboratories of Beth Israel Hospital. Mr. Trachtman now works in Washington, D.C. as a full-time lobbyist dedicated to promoting legislation that would prohibit the sale, manufacture, and installation of "No Turn on Red" signs.